MICS

AND

PANDEMICS

TRUE
STORIES

Real Tales of Deadly Diseases

JUDY DODGE CUMMINGS

Nomad Press
A division of Nomad Communications
10 9 8 7 6 5 4 3 2 1

This book was manufactured by CGB Printers,
North Mankato, Minnesota, United States
February 2018, Job #240588
ISBN Softcover: 978-1-61930-625-7
ISBN Hardcover: 978-1-61930-623-3

Educational Consultant, Marla Conn

Questions regarding the ordering of this book should be addressed to
Nomad Press
2456 Christian St.
White River Junction, VT 05001
www.nomadpress.net

Printed in the United States.

Contents

Titles in the
Mystery & Mayhem Series

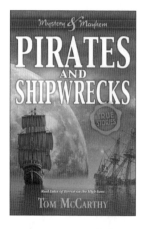

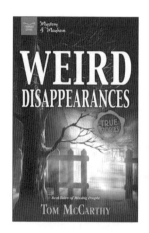

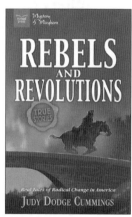

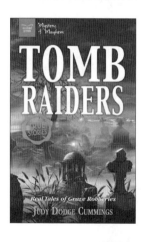

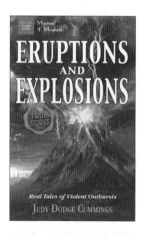

Check out more titles at www.nomadpress.net

Introduction

Bloodthirsty Bacteria and Venomous Viruses

How do you feel? Have you got the sniffles or a sore throat? If so, you might want to put this book aside until you feel better, because even if you feel okay right now, you might get a little queasy while reading.

This book is about diseases—the really bad kind of diseases. Epidemics that swept through cities, states, and countries. Epidemics that transformed into pandemics, going global and killing people from north to south and east to west.

From the earliest days of recorded history, bacteria and viruses have stalked humans. Lurking in dirty corners and sewage-filled streets, stowing away on ships and airplanes, they waited for their chance to attack.

Their deadly bite was often brushed off as the prick of a mosquito or itch of a flea. Sometimes, these villains even cloaked their menace in the kiss of a mother or embrace of a friend.

Epidemics and Pandemics

This book is about some of history's most critical contagions. First up—the "Black Death." In 1347, Europeans woke up to find tumors the size of eggs in their armpits and on their groins and necks. The bubonic plague massacred one-third of Europe's population in only five years, changing Europe's economy and social structure forever.

But those hardy Europeans bounced back, and set out to conquer the Americas in the sixteenth century. Spanish conquistador Hernán Cortés arrived in Mexico in 1518. With a few hundred soldiers, some horses and guns, he prepared to invade the mighty Aztec empire.

This task should have been impossible for the cocky Cortés, but he had a secret weapon— smallpox. The disease killed 50 percent of the Aztecs before the Spaniards even fired a shot.

Fast forward to 1793. The United States was a brand new nation brimming with optimism. Merchant ships from as far away as Africa and China anchored in the harbor of its capital city, Philadelphia, Pennsylvania. Hidden between barrels of wine and bolts of cloth in the hold of one ship was mosquito larvae infected with the yellow fever virus.

As people in the city fell sick, many wondered if the infant nation could survive it.

In 1918, as millions of men died in the trenches of France during World War I, their loved ones back home began to die, too. The Spanish influenza of 1918 struck with a speed and ferocity never seen before, killing 50 million people around the world.

In the 1980s, a mysterious illness began to affect gay men and intravenous drug users. They lost weight, developed rare infections, and died quickly and painfully. Acquired immunodeficiency syndrome (AIDS), spread through bodily fluids, was a disease ignored by the public and politicians. AIDS victims were shunned, as some people believed the disease was a punishment for leading a sinful life. But they were wrong. Anyone can get AIDS.

Today, almost 40 million people carry the virus and AIDS has killed 35 million more.

This book is full of tragic stories. These diseases killed millions of people, while fear and panic pushed some individuals to behave monstrously. But every tragedy has a hero. There were those who tended the sick, rallied their communities, and searched for a cure. Epidemics can be agents of change.

Some details might be gruesome. Some might make you wince or squirm. But to be forewarned is to be forearmed. If history is any judge, bloodthirsty bacteria and venomous viruses will return. The question is—will the world be ready?

RUSSIA

1352   MOSCOW

POLAND

1350-1351

1346-1348

FRANCE

VENICE

MARSEILLE   GENOA

CAFFA

SPAIN

FLORENCE

1346-1348

MESSINA

TURKEY   134

ALGERIA   1348-1349

1348-1349

LIBYA

EGYPT

1347–1353
The bubonic plague
spreads from the
Mediterranean
throughout Europe,
Africa, and Asia,
killing between
75 and 200
million people.

YOU
ARE
HERE

N
W   E
S

1315	1347–1353	1350s
A year of almost continual rain in Europe	Between 75 million and 200 million Europeans and Asians die from the bubonic plague in what is called the "Great Mortality"	The Renaissance begins in Europe, a cultural rebirth focused on the arts, music, and literature

Chapter One

The Great Mortality: Bubonic Plague

In the central Asian country of Kyrgyzstan, Lake Issyk Kul sits nestled in a valley surrounded by snow-capped mountains. The crisp air carries the fruity smell of spruce trees and golden beaches hug the eye-shaped lake. This peaceful setting is scarcely the place one would expect to give birth to the worst mass murderer in history.

But during the fourteenth century, just such a villain hitched a ride south and embarked on a killing spree that left millions dead. The murderer's name was *Yersinia pestis.*

Yersinia pestis is no ordinary villain—it is a bacterium.

Historians call this grim reaper the black death, or bubonic plague. People in fourteenth-century Europe referred to its five-year reign of terror as the Great Mortality.

Yersinia pestis has been around for thousands of years. It usually lives in "plague reservoirs." These are isolated parts of the world that house colonies of wild rodents, *Yersinia pestis*'s favorite host.

During the 1300s, one such reservoir was Lake Issyk Kul on the Mongolian Steppe. The tarbagan lived there. This is a species of marmot prized for its golden fur. Buried in that fur were fleas, the vector that would carry *Yersinia pestis* on a European death tour.

Yersinia pestis is a wanderer. Normally, it travels very slowly. It takes a perfect storm of circumstances for this bacterium to ignite a major outbreak of the plague.

In the mid-1300s, just such a storm occurred.

———◆———

People were on the move during the early 1300s. Nomads had created a road across the Mongolian

Steppe, and European merchants eager to trade with China discovered it. They could use this overland route to transport items east faster than by ship.

When merchants camped overnight at Lake Issyk Kul, tiny stowaways—fleas—leapt into their luggage. In the bloodstream of these fleas rode *Yersinia pestis*.

The flea could survive for six weeks without food as it traveled comfortably in a bag of grain or on a bolt of silk. When the merchant reached a city, the fleas jumped onto a secondary vector—the rat.

Rats were everywhere during the Middle Ages. Rats breed with lightning speed and they are great survivors. In three years, 329 million babies can be produced starting with just one rat couple! The rat can leap 3 feet from a standing position and drop 50 feet without injury. Rats can squeeze through a quarter-inch opening and gnaw through lead, concrete, and brick.

In the body of the flea, on the back of a rat, *Yersinia pestis* could go anywhere.

Weather was another factor that paved the way for *Yersinia pestis*'s conquest of Europe. A mini ice-age struck Europe around 1250.

Winters were cold and summers wet. Waterlogged wheat and rye rotted in the fields. There were volcanic eruptions in Italy, earthquakes in Austria, floods in Germany, and swarms of locusts in Poland.

Epidemics and Pandemics

Mother Nature was not happy during the late 1200s. These weather extremes lured *Yersinia pestis* out of hiding.

Nothing makes *Yersinia pestis* happier than death and misery, and Europe had these to spare during the early 1300s.

The cities of Venice and Genoa fought constantly for control over the seas around the Italian peninsula. France and England kicked off the Hundred Years' War, and conflicts raged from Scotland to Spain. In this bloody time, *Yersinia pestis* would thrive.

There was filth, too, a bacterium's favorite environment.

Cities were overcrowded cesspools. Barbers not only cut hair, they also cut veins. Barber-surgeons treated ill patients with a method called bloodletting. Slice a vein open. Drain some blood into a bowl. Bandage up the sick person, then dump the blood into the street.

Butchers slaughtered livestock out in the open. Piles of discarded hearts, livers, and guts attracted flies and rats. Few cities had any form of sanitation.

Laws simply required people to yell, "Look out below!" three times before emptying their chamber pots out the window.

The Quack, by Franz Anton Maulbertsch,
shows barber surgeons at work

Streets in Paris, France, were named for the
crud that clogged the gutters—rue de Pipi and rue
Merdelet, for example. "Pipi" is the French word for
pee and "merde" is French for, well . . . the other
thing.

Life in the country was better, but not without risk.
Peasants lived in mud and wattle huts with thatched
roofs infested with insects. In winter months,

livestock lived indoors with their owners. Heating water was time-consuming and costly, so people rarely bathed.

Dirt, blood, war, environmental extremes, and humans on the move created the travel package *Yersinia pestis* had been waiting for. The bacterium hit the road in the 1340s.

Its first stop was Caffa.

The medieval town of Caffa sat on the east coast of Crimea where it dips its big toe into the Black Sea. This bustling town of 70,000 people was full of merchants from Genoa, Italy. Slaves from Ukraine, sturgeons from the Don River, silk from Central Asia, and timber and fur from Russia were loaded into hundreds of galleys docked in the harbor. Once their cargo holds were full, these ships headed to ports as far away as London, England.

The Genoese governed Caffa under a grant issued by the Mongols. These were rulers of a great empire that stretched from the Yellow River in China to the Danube River in Eastern Europe. Caffa was a Mongol colony, and the Genoese and Mongol leaders often clashed.

In 1343, a major dispute broke out between Genoese merchants and local Mongols. The Genoese retreated behind the walls of Caffa, and a large Mongol army laid siege to the town. The Mongols prepared to starve the Italians out.

Three years passed, and the siege strategy might have worked but for one problem. While the Mongols' attention was glued on Caffa, *Yersinia pestis* snuck up from behind and bit the Mongols hard.

When the Genoese saw the Mongol army shrink as soldiers sickened, they were overjoyed. God had spared them!

Not so fast.

According to legend, Khan Janibeg, the Mongol leader, issued a final parting shot. He "ordered corpses to be placed in catapults and lobbed into the city in hopes that the intolerable stench would kill everyone inside. . . ."

No accounts survive to describe what life was like in Caffa after those infected Mongol bodies sailed over the city walls, but it could not have been pretty. Panicked Genoese must have surged to the harbor, desperate to escape the city of death.

As white sails unfurled and the galleys moved westward, the passengers would have breathed a sigh of relief. They had escaped. But the roar of the wind and the flap of the sails covered the squeaks of rats crawling in the cargo hold, scratching the fleas that infested their fur.

Inside those fleas lurked *Yersinia pestis*.

In late September, a fleet of Genoese galleys drifted into Sicily, the island off the boot of the Italian peninsula. As fishermen unloaded their catch and housewives gossiped from windows, dockworkers boarded the ships and unloaded the cargo in the city of Messina. The Genoese crew went ashore, unknowingly bringing their stowaway with them.

Almost immediately, the people of Messina began to sicken. Michele da Piazza, a Franciscan friar, wrote that the sailors had "such a disease in their bodies that if anyone so much as spoke with one . . . he was infected." When they realized the crew had brought a plague to town, authorities expelled the Genoese.

It was too late. *Yersinia pestis* had landed.

The plague preys on humans in many ways. Bubonic is the most common form, transmitted by a flea bite. Once *Yersinia pestis* enters the bloodstream, the bacterium drains to lymph nodes in the groin, armpit, or neck.

An infected person feels a "kind of chilly stiffness." Their body tingles as if "being pricked by the points of arrows." Next, egg-shaped tumors, or buboes, swell up over the lymph nodes. These are caused by bleeding under the skin, which turns the skin black.

A Welshman described the painful boils on his body in 1349. "It is of the form of an apple, like the head of an onion. . . . Great is its seething, like a burning cinder, a grievous thing of an ashy color."

These grotesque swellings are accompanied by a high fever, vomiting, and diarrhea. As the nervous system begins to fail, the victim's limbs move in bizarre patterns and pain ricochets through the body.

No one had ever seen an illness like this before.

Infected people not only looked like death, they reeked of it, too. One man who visited his dying friend wrote, "The stench [of] sweat, excrement, and breath was overpowering." Purplish splotches appeared on the chest and back of victims. People labeled these "God's tokens," because the marks meant death would soon follow. As horrible as the bubonic plague looked and smelled, about 40 percent of people who contracted it survived.

Determined to kill more victims, *Yersinia pestis* evolved. In some people, it managed to break out of the lymphatic system and invade the lungs. At this point, the bubonic plague became the pneumonic plague.

Victims coughed up blood, splattering *Yersinia pestis* into the air. The bacteria soared through space looking for a human to land on. If untreated, the pneumonic plague is almost 100-percent fatal.

As *Yersinia pestis* raced through Messina, the city became a ghost town. No children played on the beaches. Shopkeepers locked their doors and shuttered their windows. Church pews sat empty and streets were deserted.

Bacteria infected peoples' bodies, but fear sickened their souls. Friar Michele recorded, "Soon men hated each other so much that if a son was attacked by the disease, his father would not tend him."

The dying suffered alone, abandoned even by priests too frightened to enter the homes of the ill to hear peoples' deathbed confessions. Corpses rotted as terrified Messinians fled the city, seeking refuge across Sicily.

They unknowingly took *Yersinia pestis* along.

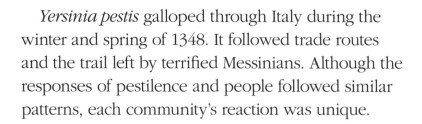

Yersinia pestis galloped through Italy during the winter and spring of 1348. It followed trade routes and the trail left by terrified Messinians. Although the responses of pestilence and people followed similar patterns, each community's reaction was unique.

When the plague arrived in the floating city of Venice in January 1348, the city's response was organized and ruthless. All ships entering the harbor were boarded and searched. Vessels with foreigners or corpses were set on fire.

In order to maintain order, Venice's city council shut down all taverns. Anyone selling liquor without permission was fined and their wine dumped into the sea.

Public gondolas navigated canals between houses each morning, crying "Bring out your dead." The convoys transported bodies to nearby islands for burial. Despite these strategies, Venice's death toll rose and morale plummeted.

In an effort to boost spirits, city leaders banned people from wearing black and pardoned imprisoned criminals. But *Yersinia pestis* was heartless. The Black Death killed 72,000 Venetians, about 60 percent of the city's population.

Hunting fresh blood, *Yersinia pestis* moved inland. Florence, the once grand city where modern banking had been invented, had fallen on hard times. In 1345, rains flooded the city. The following year brought a financial crisis. Then, in 1347, famine struck. The city wore a cloak of misery.

Nothing, however, had prepared Florence for *Yersinia pestis.*

One cloudy March morning in 1348, the pestilence crept under the city walls. Pausing momentarily, *Yersinia pestis* gazed appreciatively at Florence's stunning art and architecture. Then, it pounced.

Florentine writer Giovanni Boccaccio recorded *Yersinia pestis*'s visit. "It would rush upon its victims with the speed of a fire racing through dry or oily substances. . . ."

The plague's speed heightened peoples' terror until it became a hysteria. The healthy ran from the sick. According to Boccaccio, "Brothers abandon brothers, uncles their nephews, sisters their brothers, and . . . wives deserted husbands. But even worse . . . fathers and mothers refused to nurse . . . their own children."

Florence's famous beauty vanished, replaced by a mask of death.

People dropped dead in the street, their bodies left where they had fallen. A rank odor coming from windows notified passersby that someone in the neighborhood had died. Huge burial trenches were dug in churchyards. Marchionne di Coppo Stefani described how corpses were dropped into these pits, "layer upon layer just like one puts layers of cheese on lasagna."

An eerie silence fell over Florence. This was a city full of churches, and in normal times, the bells pealed three times a day, plus when someone died.

An illustration from a fourteenth-century
Belgium manuscript, author unknown

When *Yersinia pestis* turned these death chimes
into a continuous clang, the city council ordered the
bells silenced. But the end of the music did not stop
Yersinia pestis from killing.

The Great Mortality claimed 50,000 Florentines
before it left the city—50 percent of the population.
Europeans were desperate for a cure.

◆

Medieval medicine was based as much on
superstition and tradition as on science. European
doctors relied on theories that had been developed
by the ancient Greeks centuries earlier.

Few doctors had formal training and the scientific
method did not yet exist.

Epidemics and Pandemics

In 1348, desperate to understand what caused *Yersinia pestis*, doctors at the University of Paris wrote the *Compendium de Epidemia*. They concluded the plague was caused by bad air. Their theory was based on astrology.

The scientists had observed that on March 20, 1345, three planets in the Aquarius constellation were aligned. One of these, Mars, was "a malevolent planet, breeding anger and wars. . . ." and it "looked upon Jupiter with a hostile aspect."

The alignment of these planets sucked up "evil vapors," which winds carried to Earth. When inhaled, bad air can "penetrate quickly to the heart and lungs to do its damage."

This explanation was little help since Europeans could not just hold their breath until *Yersinia pestis* left town. Instead, doctors proposed creative, although not successful, solutions. Stay away from marshes and swamps, where the air was thick. Open north-facing windows to let in the dry air. Cover up windows that face the hot, humid south.

The physician John Colle noted that the people who cleaned public latrines seemed less likely to contract the plague than the general population. Therefore, Colle argued, the best cure for bad air was more bad air. This theory led people to circle around public outhouses and inhale deeply.

Sniffing latrines was not the only treatment for this terrifying disease.

People ate crushed emeralds, chopped up raw onions and scattered them around the house, and drank their own urine. They placed live pigeons or frogs on the boils and covered burst buboes with poultices that included figs, butter, onions, and dried human feces. None of these "cures" halted *Yersinia pestis*'s murderous march through Europe.

———◆———

When Italy had been decimated, *Yersinia pestis* decided to try French food.

The southern coastal city of Marseille became an urban hub from which the disease could wrap a hangman's noose around the entire continent.

Southwest to Spain, north toward England, a sharp right into the Low Countries, and from there to Scandinavia, Germany, Poland, and finally Russia by 1352. The only European countries *Yersinia pestis* spared were Iceland and Finland. These nations likely escaped because they had small populations and little contact with the rest of Europe.

While Europeans died by the millions, a manhunt began. This search for *Yersinia pestis* was not led by doctors or scientists. It was led by anti-Semites— people who discriminate against Jewish people.

April 13, 1348, was Palm Sunday, the beginning of Holy Week for European Christians. That evening, Christian residents of the seaside village of Toulon, France, attacked their Jewish neighbors.

As darkness fell, mobs burst into Jewish houses. Crazed people broke windows and overturned furniture. They dragged Jewish men, women, and children from bed, hauling them into the streets, where they were taunted, beaten, and killed.

The following morning, the bodies of 40 Jews hung from poles in the town square.

Anti-Semitism had long roots in Europe. The majority of the population was Christian, and they blamed the Jewish minority for the death of Jesus, the Christian messiah. Jesus was executed by Romans in the Jewish holy city of Jerusalem back in 33 CE.

The Christian church dominated Europe, its rules as powerful as those of any monarch. These rules applied to Jews even though they practiced a different religion. Jews had to wear distinctive clothing, such as yellow badges or red hats. They were barred from owning land and practicing certain occupations. Some towns refused to allow any Jewish residents, and many cities required Jews to live in a walled-off section known as a ghetto.

Already viewed as separate and suspect, the Jews made an easy scapegoat during a crisis.

As *Yersinia pestis* raced across northern Europe, rumor sprinted ahead of it. The plague, people whispered, was part of an international Jewish conspiracy to take over the world.

"The Jews have poisoned Christian wells," a shopkeeper said to a shoemaker. "The poison is the size of an egg," the shoemaker said to the mayor. "Nay," said the mayor. "The size of a fist." "I heard it was as big as two fists," whispered a housewife.

This two-fisted poison was rumored to be made of lizards. Or was it frogs and spiders?

No, claimed the most devilish rumor—the Jewish poison contained the hearts of Christians.

This gossip spread across France, Germany, and Switzerland like a herald in advance of *Yersinia pestis*. Jews were arrested and hauled before authorities to be "put to the question," another phrase for torture. If the person did not confess to being part of the conspiracy, a guard placed a crown of thorns on his head and smashed it into his skull with a club. Jews quickly "admitted" to being part of the poison plot. They lied simply to end the torture.

Such a conspiracy never existed.

Yersinia pestis targeted Jewish Europeans as viciously as their Christian neighbors. That fact did not matter to the Christians who beat Jews with spikes. An estimated 20,000 European Jews died during the Great Mortality, slain by the two demons of pestilence and prejudice.

◆

In 1352, *Yersinia pestis* reached Moscow, Russia, and gnawed through the population with deadly speed. Then, this mass murderer pushed back its plate and decided it was full. Moscow is approximately 700 miles from Caffa, the city where the Great Mortality had begun.

When Europeans realized the plague had gone, they celebrated. Men and women drank and spent money. They had survived the apocalypse and embraced life with gusto.

But *Yersinia pestis* had altered their world. The church had failed them. Prayer had not saved them. People became skeptical of church authority and were open to considering different religious ideas.

The economy went through a fundamental shift after *Yersinia pestis* left town. Fields lay unplanted, farms abandoned, fences and bridges fell apart. There were not enough laborers to tend the land. Peasants who had survived the plague no longer had to take dirt wages offered by upper-class landowners. They demanded more money and began to purchase their own land and fight for more rights.

Medicine evolved as well. No longer were doctors content to rely on theories developed during ancient times. They began to propose new ideas and test these concepts with observable and measurable data. The scientific method was born.

Although Europe changed, these changes did not keep *Yersinia pestis* away forever. Like the villain in a horror movie, it returned in 1361. For the next 300 years, waves of the plague rolled over the continent. The death toll was never as high as it had been during the Great Mortality, but *Yersinia pestis* refused to disappear.

According to the World Health Organization, from 2010 through 2015 there were 3,248 cases of two different kinds of plague in humans, and 584 of these people died. Though tragic, these numbers pale in comparison to the slaughter of the fourteenth century. Antibiotics and improved hygiene and sanitation keep the monster in check—but never forget that it is still around. Anyone planning to travel to a place where rats and marmots thrive should heed this warning: *Be vigilant.* Yersinia pestis *lurks inside these rodents' fur, waiting for the chance to strike again.*

LAKE TEXCOC

TEXCOCO

TENOCHTITLÁN

1519–1521

Spanish conquistador
Hernán Cortés
conquers the Aztecs
through warfare
and smallpox.

YOU
ARE
HERE

N
W · E
S

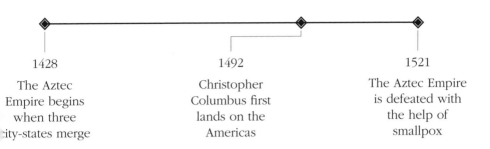

Chapter Two

Secret Weapon: Smallpox in the New World

The Aztec Empire had a lot going for it in the early sixteenth century. It was brutal, bloodthirsty, powerful, technologically advanced, and ruled by Montezuma, a god-king. So, in 1519, when Spanish conquistador Hernán Cortés decided his band of soldiers could take down the mighty Aztecs, it was a pretty nervy move.

But this is not a story about how Cortés got his conquistador's hat handed to him. Quite the opposite.

Cortés was wily and experienced, as well as being fired-up to steal land and gold for King Charles V of Spain and convert the natives of Mexico to Christianity. Spanish soldiers wore armor, rode horses, and carried guns, three technological advances the Aztecs lacked.

Still, Montezuma would have wiped his Mexican tile floor with Cortés but for the Spaniard's secret weapon—smallpox. With the help of this teeny, tiny, very deadly virus, Cortés brought the mighty Aztec empire to its knees. How did a disease win a war?

Smallpox, also known as *Variola major*, has been around for centuries. Scientists think that we have livestock to thank for this disease. In the past, Europeans lived close to their farm animals. Some peasants even brought cattle and sheep into their cottages on cold winter nights. This cozy arrangement was the perfect environment for an animal virus to evolve and jump species, going from killing cows to killing humans.

By the sixteenth century, smallpox visited Europe regularly. The virus targeted the young, killing about 30 percent of those infected. But if you survived, you became immune forever.

You never got the disease again.

The native people of the Americas did not have cows or horses or sheep sleeping in their homes. Therefore, the New World had no smallpox. When Cortés came knocking on the Aztecs' front door, he introduced smallpox into a population where no one had immunity.

———◆———

Sixteenth-century European monarchs were obsessed with gaining wealth and power. The best way to do both was to conquer territory. That way, they could establish colonies.

In 1492, Christopher Columbus sailed to the Caribbean and claimed the island of Hispaniola for Spain. Other explorers followed on his heels. As a kid, Cortés was fascinated by tales of gold flowing like water from the heart of mountains on Caribbean islands. In 1504, at age 19, Cortés joined an expedition to Hispaniola. He aided fellow Spaniard Diego Velázquez de Cuéllar in capturing Cuba. In return, Velázquez granted Cortés land and slaves.

But in a story as old as time, the two men fought over a woman. Although they patched up their relationship, neither really trusted the other ever again.

By 1519, Velázquez was the governor of Cuba. After much begging, Velázquez agreed to let Cortés lead an expedition to Mexico to explore land recently discovered by Europeans. Cortés was supposed to find gold, establish trade routes, and return with native peoples to use as slaves in Cuba's silver mines.

But then Velázquez called off the expedition, worried that Cortés would keep any wealth he discovered for himself. Cortés ignored Velázquez's command to stay put and sailed for Mexico anyway.

Hernán Cortés

This move would come back to bite him later.

At the end of March 1519, Cortés anchored his fleet on Mexico's northern coast. Warriors from the Tabascan tribe greeted these strangers by raining arrows, spears, and stones down on the Spaniards' heads. So Cortés brought out his cannons and cavalry. The natives had never experienced gunpowder or horses before. Soon, 800 warriors lay dead.

The next day, Tabascan representatives arrived at Cortés's camp, gifts in hand. They bore corn cakes, fruit, and a shield adorned with gold rings. Cortés eyed the gold rings.

He was in the right place.

The Tabascans said a representative from their ruler, Montezuma, would soon come to meet the Spanish. Montezuma was only five years older than Cortés, but he came from a different world. For close to 20 years, Montezuma had ruled Mexico, a triple alliance of the city-states of Tenochtitlán, Texcoco, and Tacuba—today known as the Aztecs.

He was the sole ruler of an empire that controlled most of Mexico and Central America. The capital city was Tenochtitlán, present-day Mexico City.

Nobody messed with Montezuma. People believed he was half-god. The Aztec religion was full of rituals with offerings to keep their many gods happy. These offerings included birds, flowers, food—and human hearts and blood.

The Aztecs believed the gods controlled the entire universe. If the gods grew angry, the rain wouldn't fall, the crops wouldn't grow, and the sun wouldn't rise. Therefore, to save the many, a few humans must be sacrificed. All conquered people who lived in the Aztec realm had to pay taxes to Montezuma. Some payments were in goods, some in gold, and some in victims to be sacrificed.

On Easter Sunday 1519, an ambassador from King Montezuma arrived in the Spanish camp. The man's name was Tendile and he presented Cortés with gifts made from fancy feathers and gold. Cortés decided the time had come to send a message to this mysterious Montezuma, so he put on a show.

The Spanish cavalry charged back and forth, armor glinting, swords flashing, and horses snorting. Artillerymen fired cannons at an earsplitting close range. Spanish greyhounds, never seen in the New World, raced up and down the beach, their massive tongues dangling from their huge, drooling mouths.

Tendile must have been a little freaked out. The Aztecs believed in a prophecy that said the serpent god, Quetzalcoatl, returned to Mexico every 52 years. In a bizarre coincidence, the day Cortés arrived in Mexico was the exact date the Aztec calendar predicted Quetzalcoatl would return.

The prophecy also had a dark side. It foretold that one day, Quetzalcoatl would come to "shake the foundation of heaven" and "conquer Tenochtitlán." Now, Tendile's gaze fixed on the helmet of a Spanish cavalryman. The head covering looked just like the one Quetzalcoatl wore in the Aztec art.

Cortés urged Tendile to take the helmet to show Montezuma, as long as he returned it full of gold. "I and my companions suffer from a disease of the heart," Cortés explained, "which can be cured only with gold."

Ten days later, Tendile returned with the conquistador's cure. Gold and silver plates as "large as a wagon wheel," gold necklaces, and bracelets studded with gems, golden figurines, and the helmet—full of gold flakes and nuggets.

Montezuma was pleased to offer these gifts, Tendile said, and the Spanish were free to visit the coast *for a while.* But Montezuma would not come to meet Cortés and the Spanish should not travel inland.

The message was clear. Take your gold and buzz off.

Cortés smiled and told Tendile that he simply could not leave Mexico until he had met Montezuma. Cortés intended to seize a kingdom with such treasures as this. In August 1519, Cortés led his army into Mexico's interior. Along the way, he wooed some Aztec allies and slaughtered others.

Montezuma decided he had better figure out if this white guy was man or god. He invited Cortés to visit him at Tenochtitlán. Cortés was thrilled. He had soldiers, firearms, and horses. Once inside the city, he would subdue the Aztecs and grab their gold.

❖

On November 8, 1519, Cortés stood on the bank of Lake Texcoco and stared at Tenochtitlán. The sight must have blown his mind. The Aztec capital was an island city made by architectural geniuses.

A long brick causeway led from the mainland across Lake Texcoco to Tenochtitlán. This dirt and rubble platform was 25 feet wide and 5 miles long.

Stationed at intervals along the causeway were removable wooden bridges. These bridges were the key to the city's security. If an enemy attacked, the Aztecs could lift the bridges off the causeway and toss them into the lake. Invaders could not pass the large gap in the road unless they swam across.

Tenochtitlan's stone towers and temples seemed to rise straight out of the water. Edible garden islands floated along the canals, drawing nutrients from the water. One soldier recorded that Tenochtitlán "seemed like an enchanted vision."

A procession approached the Spaniards. Four attendants carried a gold litter covered in a curtain of quetzal feathers and lined with silver and gold. The attendants set the litter down and the curtain parted. A lean man with short black hair stepped out.

Cortés had to hand it to Montezuma—the king looked good. He wore a brilliant green quetzal feather headdress, gold-bottomed sandals, and a loin cloth made from jaguar skin. Jade and blue stones studded his ears and lower lip.

Montezuma probably didn't think much of Cortés's style. The Spaniard's face bristled with a full beard and he looked battle-worn. The white skin of his face and arms bore scars. Montezuma leaned forward and sniffed Cortés. This was not a typical greeting back in Europe, and maybe Cortés took a step back. Then he remembered his manners and reached out to hug Montezuma. But two Aztec nobles stepped forward and stopped Cortes. No one touched the king.

Through a translator, Cortés asked, "Are you Montezuma?"

"Yes, I am he," the king replied.

The pair exchanged gifts, and Montezuma urged the Spaniards to go to their quarters and rest.

"We are your friends," Cortés replied. Within a week, Montezuma would learn this was a bold-faced lie.

———◆———

For several days, the Spaniards roamed the city. The marketplace was filled with butcher stands, pottery stalls, chocolate shops, stuffed birds, live birds, plucked birds, jaguar hides, golden-scaled fish, and lifelike toy monkeys. Montezuma lived in a 100-room palace. Intricate paintings covered the walls and ceilings, while stoves warmed every corner and hallways were perfumed. The heart of Tenochtitlán housed temples to the Aztec gods.

Cortés asked to see the Great Temple, and Montezuma reluctantly led him up the pyramid's 114 steps. The shrine on top was dedicated to Huitzilopochtli, the god of war and sacrifice. Signs of the 12 children who had been sacrificed when the Spanish arrived in the city were still visible. The metallic scent of blood was so strong, Cortés could almost taste it.

Cortés asked if his men could have a chapel to worship their own god in the Palace of Axayacatl, where they were being housed. Aztec masons and carpenters quickly constructed a small room for this.

When the workmen cleared out, one of the Spaniards discovered a plastered-over door in one of the chapel walls. The men pried it open and discovered a hall full of treasure. Soldier Bernal Diaz said, "It seemed to me as if all the riches of the world were in that room." Cortés ordered his men to put everything back. They must bide their time. When the city was theirs, they would divide the plunder.

———◆———

A messenger arrived from the Spanish fort on the coast with bad news. A local native chief, one of Montezuma's allies, had ambushed the Spaniards,

killing seven of them. Cortés had been "thinking of all the ways and means of capturing Montezuma without causing a disturbance." Now, he had an excuse.

On November 14, Cortés took 30 armed men to Montezuma's palace. There, he accused Montezuma of ordering his ally to attack the Spanish.

Montezuma instructs the people to lay down their arms.
painting by: Margaret Duncan Coxhead

If Montezuma agreed to come into Spanish custody quietly, the Spaniards would treat him well. But if he resisted, Cortés would kill him on the spot.

Montezuma denied ordering the ambush, but, realizing his life was on the line, he agreed to accompany the Spanish if they pretended he was doing so willingly. Montezuma told his family and advisers he was going to live with the Spanish for a while to learn their customs.

Cortés had just carried out a bold and bloodless revolt. But the fight for the empire was far from over.

———◆———

A few weeks later, the chief who had ambushed the Spanish on the coast arrived in Tenochtitlán with a dozen other leaders from that region. Cortés ordered them burned on the stake over a bonfire made of Montezuma's personal stash of swords, bows, arrows and shields. He forced the king to witness his countrymen go up in flames.

Montezuma's spirit broke. He swore allegiance to the Spanish and gave up his lands and tribute payments. All wealth that poured into the treasury was now under Cortés's control.

Fury seethed just below the city's surface. Cortés knew his grasp on Tenochtitlán was fragile.

Before he could tighten his hold on the city, a message arrived from the coast. A Spaniard from Cuba came with a mission—to capture or kill Cortés.

Here is where smallpox reenters the story. Remember Diego Velázquez, the friend-turned-enemy who cancelled Cortés's expedition to Mexico? Velázquez got wind of the riches Cortés discovered in Mexico, and he was determined to get his hands on them. He sent a fleet under the command of Pánfilo de Narváez to get Cortés.

On one of Narváez's ships was an African porter named Francisco de Eguia.

Eguia was a slave, so he probably didn't carry much luggage to Mexico, but he did carry smallpox. Eguia had been exposed to the virus in Cuba. The symptoms of smallpox don't show up for a week or two, just long enough for Eguia to sail to Mexico. After he arrived, he moved in with some locals and abruptly got sick.

Eguia was burning up and so tired he could barely lift his hand. His head and back throbbed. More than likely, a woman in the house tended the slave, bringing him broth and wiping the spittle from his mouth. Perhaps this woman later prepared food for her husband and kissed her children goodnight.

She could not have known that she had just killed her family.

Next, a rash appeared on Eguia's body. First, it sprang up in his mouth and throat, then on his palms and the soles of his feet. Soon, his entire body was covered. These pustules leaked contagious fluid into his blankets and clothes. Perhaps that same woman washed Eguia's clothes—or maybe by that time she had fallen ill herself.

The secret weapon had been fired.

From May to September, the virus slowly spread inland. Unlike in Europe, where smallpox was a childhood disease, everyone in Mexico, from the elderly to infants, fell sick at once. While the Aztecs died by the thousands, the Spaniards remained healthy because of their childhood immunity.

———◆———

Cortés did not think about smallpox as he contemplated his next move. He needed to guard Montezuma and the treasure while also dealing with Narváez. So Cortés split his forces, leaving 120 soldiers in Tenochtitlán under the command of Pedro de Alvarado and taking the rest to the coast.

A few weeks later, Cortés surprised Narváez's forces at dawn. Within an hour, Cortés had defeated his countrymen.

He lost only two men, while Narváez lost 15 and one of his eyeballs when it was impaled on a pike. But Cortés had no time to celebrate. A message arrived from Pedro de Alvarado—the Aztecs in Tenochtitlán were in rebellion.

Cortés raced back over the mountains and into the Valley of Mexico. He did not know it, but this time he carried a weapon to Tenochtitlán more deadly than any musket. Smallpox.

As soon as Cortés had left Tenochtitlán, Pedro de Alvarado became jumpy. Afraid the Aztecs were planning an uprising, Alvarado struck first.

During a religious festival, thousands of Aztecs crowded into the Patio of Dances to watch the Serpent Dance. The best warriors sported headdresses of quetzal feathers and cloaks of puma skins as they danced to drums and flutes. As the music grew louder and the dancers fell into a religious trance, Alvarado bellowed, "Let them die!"

In minutes, all that remained in the Patio of Dances were piles of dead nobles. Messengers raced through the city. "Mexicanos, come running! Bring your spears and shields. The strangers have murdered our warriors!"

The Spanish retreated to their quarters, bolting the doors and windows. They had the firepower to hold their ground, but with no food or water, they would not last long. As Alvarado lay on his pallet that night, he prayed Cortés would return soon to save them.

———◆———

Cortés reached Tenochtitlán on June 24, 1520, with a force of 3,000. The city was a ghost town. The Aztecs were mourning for those murdered during the Serpent Dance.

In the Palace of Axayacatl, Cortés found his thin and shriveled soldiers with the still-captive king. He ordered Montezuma to tell his people to reopen the market so the Spaniards could get food.

Montezuma shrugged. The people wouldn't listen to him anymore. Perhaps his brother, Cuitláhuac, could convince them, he offered. Cortés agreed, and Cuitláhuac, who had been held captive with Montezuma, was set free. Cortés would regret it.

Cuitláhuac went directly to the few surviving nobles and enlisted their help. The men stripped all power from Montezuma and named Cuitláhuac the new king. They kept the market closed, raised the causeways leading to Tenochtitlán, and marched thousands of warriors to the Sacred Precinct.

Cuitláhuac was going to war.

For a week, the fighting raged. The Spaniards rained firepower down from the roof of their palace quarters and the Aztecs died by the hundreds. But for every man killed, 10 more took his place.

Cortés tried one, last-ditch effort at diplomacy. He told Montezuma to climb to the rooftop and tell his people to lay down their arms.

"I wish only to die," Montezuma said.

Soldiers dragged the former king to the roof and ordered him to speak. Whatever Montezuma said was swallowed by the angry roar of the crowd. Stones soared over the roof and arrows cut through the sky. Montezuma was struck in the head and chest. The soldiers covered him with their shields and ran for cover.

Montezuma died on June 30, 1520, killed by his own people.

Cortés knew it was time to escape. He took a large chunk of Montezuma's treasure for himself and then told his men to fill their bags with whatever they could carry. Then, just after midnight on July 1, the Spaniards and their allies fled Tenochtitlán.

Rain fell and the streets were deserted as they stepped on the causeway. When the group reached the first breach in the bridge, Cortés ordered his men to lay down the portable bridge they had made.

Suddenly, a cry broke the night. "Mexicanos!" a woman wailed. "Our enemies are escaping!"

In minutes, the lake was thick with canoes filled with warriors. The Spaniards were stretched out single file on the causeway and could not defend themselves. So many Spaniards fell into the gap in the bridge that the Aztecs said, "Those who followed crossed to the other side by walking on the corpses."

As dawn peeked over the horizon, the survivors stumbled to the outskirts of Tacuba, a nearby city. Six hundred Spanish soldiers and 4,000 of their Tlaxcalan allies had been killed. The treasure they had tried to steal lay at the bottom of Lake Texcoco. The Spaniards called the catastrophe La Noche Triste—the Night of Sorrows.

The Spanish sorrows were nothing compared to the tragedy about to envelop Tenochtitlán. Cortés had left behind his secret weapon and it began to kill.

The Aztecs repaired their temples and scrubbed blood from the city streets. They rebuilt their causeways and celebrated their festivals. But just as life began to return to normal, people fell mysteriously ill.

Flaming pustules that the Aztecs called the "Great Rash" broke out all over their bodies.

Some people were so covered in blisters that they did not look human. Others got blisters on their eyes and became blind. Victims lay on their beds like living corpses, unable to even roll from one side to another. Entire families fell ill at the same time.

There was no one healthy enough to make food or wash dirty sheets or bathe fevered brows. People who might have survived the virus died from exposure, starvation, or secondary infections.

Doctors used ancient remedies to treat this unknown illness. Powdered obsidian was pasted on a victim's oozing sores. Bloodstone was applied to the nostrils. Herbal teas and crushed beetles were consumed. Nothing helped. So many people died there was not time for funerals. Canoes full of corpses were emptied into the middle of Lake Texcoco.

In just two months, tens of thousands of Aztecs died. When smallpox had killed all it could in Tenochtitlán, it moved through the rest of the Aztec empire and kept traveling north and south. In some communities, half of the population died.

———◆———

After La Noche Triste, the Spaniards sought refuge in Tlaxcala among native allies. They remained there for several months while the wounded recovered.

This included Cortés, who had suffered a fractured skull and two crushed fingers. His immunity from smallpox gave him power. Cortés wrote to King Charles of Spain that, "Many chieftains were dying and they wished . . . that by my hand . . . others might be put in their place." So Cortés handpicked the chiefs who would back him against the Aztecs.

Despite the loss of so many men, the conquistador refused to give up his dream of conquering Tenochtitlán. Cortés concocted a bold plan to storm Tenochtitlán by water. Spanish carpenters built a fleet of brigantines. These 40-foot-long sailing ships were hauled in pieces over the mountains to the city of Texcoco, a journey of 50 miles.

Normally a city of 15,000 people, only 600 survivors of smallpox remained in Texcoco. These pathetic survivors surrendered to the Spanish.

The ships were pieced together, and an army of laborers dug a mile-long canal, 12 feet deep and 12 feet wide. Rains fell, the canal filled, and on April 28, 1521, Cortés began the siege of Tenochtitlán.

While Cortés had been plotting, building, marching, and digging, the people of Tenochtitlán had been mourning. On December 4, 1520, smallpox had claimed King Cuitláhuac, Montezuma's brother.

For two months, the empire had no ruler. Chiefs in neighboring areas also died from smallpox. As new men took their places, and with no emperor to demand their loyalty, Cortés stepped in. Some allied with the Spaniards out of fear, others because they were sick of paying tribute to the Aztecs.

By the time Cortés was ready to attack Tenochtitlán, he commanded an army of 200,000 native allies.

Finally, Prince Cuauhtémoc, the nephew of Montezuma and Cuitláhuac, was inaugurated as king in February 1521. When this battle-hardened 25-year-old tried to secure allies among the surrounding tribes, he found that most chiefs had already cast their lot with Cortés.

The first target of the Spanish was the Chapultepec aqueduct. This 2-mile pipe funneled spring water from a hillside town into the center of Tenochtitlán. It was the city's lifeline. The Spaniards seized the spring, cutting off water to Tenochtitlán.

In early June, the Spanish and Aztecs engaged in a naval battle on Lake Texcoco. The Aztec canoes were nimble, but they were no match for the brigantines, which launched headfirst into the Aztec canoes with cannons blasting. One survivor said, "So many were killed that all of the great lake was so stained with blood that it did not look like water."

But the Aztecs weren't giving up. On June 10, Cortés assaulted the center of the city. He was driven back not once, not twice, but three times over the next several days. This was how strong the city was even after being decimated by smallpox. If the Spaniards had not brought the disease to Mexico, Cortés probably never would have made it past Tenochtitlan's front gates.

The siege wore on. By day, the Spaniards filled in gaps in the causeways and by night, the Aztecs tore them open again. Rain fell daily. The Spaniards lived in their dank, smelly armor and survived on maize cakes, cherries, and herbs. The soldiers' morale was slipping.

Their mood worsened after a disastrous attempt to capture the market on June 30.

The raid failed and 70 Spaniards were captured alive and taken to the Great Temple. From the safety of the other side of the causeway, the Spaniards watched their countrymen being sacrificed.

King Cuauhtémoc sent messengers to his former allies in neighboring cities. The Spaniards are almost defeated, he crowed. Severed heads and amputated limbs of the Spanish prisoners were shown as proof.

Many natives deserted Cortés's camp and King Cuauhtémoc predicted in eight days, all Spaniards would be dead

◆

King Cuauhtémoc was wrong. The Spaniards hung on and the Aztecs grew weaker. Still weak from the smallpox epidemic, they now suffered from hunger and thirst. The "stagnant . . . brine of the lake" was the only drinking water in the city. The only food was lizards, swallows, corncobs, and grass. To fill their bellies, people chewed deer hides and ate dirt.

On the evening of August 12, 1521, a "great bonfire" wheeled across the sky. It shot sparks and rumbled and hissed over Lake Texcoco before abruptly vanishing. For the superstitious Aztecs, this celestial object—a comet or shooting star—was an omen. Their gods had forsaken them.

The next day, King Cuauhtémoc was caught as he tried to flee across the lake in a canoe.

"Ah, Captain," he said when brought before Cortés, "I have already done everything in my power to defend my kingdom. . . . And since my fortune has not been favorable, take my life."

It was August 13, 1521.

The day the Aztec Empire ended.

Cortés did not kill King Cuauhtémoc. Instead, he allowed the surviving Aztecs to leave the city. Then, he torched the king's feet until Cuauhtémoc revealed the location of the Aztec gold and silver.

It had all been tossed into Lake Texcoco.

Teams of Spanish divers searched, but they recovered little. Cortés ordered Tenochtitlán destroyed, down to every last home and temple.

Smallpox did not stop killing once the Spanish were in charge. The secret weapon that was no longer secret struck over and over and was joined by other European diseases, such as mumps and measles. According to one estimate, between 1518 and the early 1600s, roughly 100 million native peoples died from European diseases. This was one-fifth of the world's population.

Communities reduced and ravaged by disease could not withstand European conquerors. By the seventeenth century, the great Indian empires of North and South America had disappeared. Europeans were firmly in power. The smallest weapon in the arsenal of Hernán Cortés proved to be the most powerful one of all—powerful enough to alter history.

NEW YORK

VERMONT

NEW HAMPS

MASSACHUSE

CONNECTICU

PENNSYLVANIA

RHO
ISL

PHILADELPHIA ★

NEW JER

MARYLAND

DELAWARE

WASHINGTON, DC ★

VIRGINIA

ATLANT
OCEAN

1793
Philadelphia's bout of yellow fever nearly cripples the fledgling nation of the United States and contributes to the establishment of a board of public health.

YOU
ARE
HERE

N
W   E
S

1783	1793	1900
The United States wins its independence from Great Britain	A yellow fever epidemic breaks out in Philadelphia, threatening the process of building a government	Dr. Walter Reed finally proves mosquitoes cause yellow fever

Chapter Three

Yellow Fever Threatens Independence

Mosquitoes are a fact of life in the summer, but this tiny pest also carries the virus that is one of history's worst killers. In 1793, Philadelphia, Pennsylvania, was a city on the rise. Only 10 years earlier, the United States had won the war of independence against the British Empire, and the metropolis of 50,000 people was named the new nation's capital. But that August, an epidemic of yellow fever carried by mosquitoes turned Philadelphia into a gruesome graveyard.

To understand the impact of the yellow fever epidemic, you need to see Philadelphia in the days before disaster struck. The tour begins at the waterfront, the heart of the city.

Merchants from as far away as China sail up the Delaware River to unload their cargo at Philadelphia's docks. You can eavesdrop on shipowners arguing with ship captains and watch broad-shouldered dockworkers hoist barrels and crates. Watch as another ship arrives from the French island of Santo Domingo, bringing refugees. Some 2,000 have come since July, desperate to escape the violent slave uprising on Santo Domingo.

Water Street parallels the Delaware River. Follow it to find warehouses, boardinghouses, and grog shops aplenty. But the seagulls here are likely to drop something disgusting on your head, so let's stroll up High Street. The cobblestone streets are full of wagons and carts today—watch your feet!

These three blocks of High Street are the market district. Vegetables, fresh fish, a leg of lamb—buy whatever suits you. There are many wild pigeons for sale today. Some people believe too many pigeons means a sickness is in the air.

Mind yourself! You don't want to fall into that "sink." A sink is the eighteenth-century equivalent of a sewer. No pipes or cover, just a deep hole to collect runoff or dead cats or a rotten onion. You'll find these all over the city.

Inhale deeply. Strong cheese, fish guts, horse manure, and sewage. That's history you smell.

If you keep walking down High Street, you might catch a glimpse of President George Washington. Philadelphia is the headquarters of the federal government, so the first president lives just a few blocks away.

Philadelphia had a rainy spring. You can see pools of water in the alleys, and the water barrels people keep in their yards are still brimming. Look closely in those barrels and you'll see mosquito eggs hatching.

Watch out! There's a mosquito on your arm. You don't want to get bit. Otherwise, you might never find out what happened to Philadelphia when yellow fever struck in August of 1793.

———◆———

The virus-carrying mosquitoes were stowaways.

The ships bringing refugees to Philadelphia from Santo Domingo carried water casks. Mosquitoes stowed away inside these casks and laid eggs. The eggs hatched and the mosquitoes did what mosquitoes do—they bit people. One of the ship's passengers had been infected with yellow fever back on Santo Domingo and one person was all it took.

Yellow fever is an arboviral disease. That means it's transmitted to humans by a vector, in this case an insect that carries the virus.

Yellow fever's vector is *Aedes aegypti,* a mosquito that originated in Africa. After the bug bites an infected person, the virus reproduces in the mosquito's gut. Then, it moves up to the insect's salivary glands and is ready for action.

As soon as the bug bites its next victim, the yellow fever virus is injected into the person's bloodstream. The female mosquito can also pass the virus through its infected eggs. These eggs lay dormant during dry conditions, but give them a little water and bam!

They're hatched and hungry.

Yellow fever probably originated in the rainforests of Africa. As villages developed, *Aedes aegypti* discovered they liked human blood and urban life. By the 1500s, slave ships traveled regularly between West Africa and the Caribbean, and *Aedes aegypti* hopped on board, probably as eggs in a water cask.

A few days out of port, the eggs hatched, lunched on slaves and crew, and then laid more eggs. When the ship reached its destination, both infected people and virus-carrying vectors disembarked together.

Yellow fever appeared in Mexico in 1648, and by 1693, it had reached colonial America. The virus struck cities regularly in the summer months until 1765, when it disappeared from North American cities for almost 30 years.

In 1793, yellow fever returned—with a vengeance.

—————◆—————

On August 3, a French sailor living on Water Street came down with a high fever. In a couple days, he was dead.

On August 4, Polly Lear, the wife of President Washington's secretary, died.

On August 5, Dr. Benjamin Rush was called to the house of Hugh Hodge, a fellow physician. Hodge's daughter was throwing up black blood and her skin had turned yellow. She died that afternoon.

Rush felt a twinge of alarm. In the last few days, he had treated "an unusual number of bilious fevers," and believed "all was not right in our city." During the next two weeks, Rush attended 10 more people who all lived in the Water Street neighborhood and had similar symptoms: high fever, yellow skin, bleeding from the nose and gums, and vomiting black blood.

On August 19, Rush met with two other doctors at the home of Peter La Maigre, a French importer whose wife was sick. The La Maigres lived on the waterfront near Ball's Wharf. Recently, a ship had arrived with a cargo of rotten coffee. The beans had been dumped on the wharf and were decomposing in the hot sun.

Rush concluded a "bilious yellow fever" was killing Catherine La Maigre, and the stench from the coffee was causing it.

◆

When Benjamin Rush issued a diagnosis, people listened. He was the most respected doctor in Philadelphia. Rush had served in the First Continental Congress in 1776, signed the Declaration of Independence, and been surgeon general of the Continental Army during the Revolutionary War.

After the war, Dr. Rush opened up a private practice and was a member of Philadelphia's College of Physicians. Rush recognized the symptoms of yellow fever, because when he was an apprentice in 1762, he worked under a doctor who treated patients with the disease.

Catherine La Maigre died on August 20, along with six other Philadelphians. The next day, 12 more died, and the day after that, another 13. These victims did not all live on the waterfront. The fever was moving.

Rush warned Philly's mayor, Matthew Clarkson, that a yellow fever epidemic had struck the city. Clarkson printed a notice in the newspapers to inform the public "that a dangerous infectious disorder" was on the loose. He also called a meeting of the College of Physicians.

Surely, the city's top physicians could stop this epidemic in its tracks.

———◆———

Doctors in 1793 were still playing by a rulebook written in ancient times. The words "germs," "bacteria," and "virus" had not even been invented. Physicians believed sickness was caused by body fluids being out of whack. The four body fluids were blood, phlegm, black bile, and yellow bile. Too much of one or too little of another made you sick. Doctors spent less time peering down your throat than they did examining your poop, pee, puke, and blood.

Philadelphia's doctors argued about what caused yellow fever. Rush and some doctors blamed it on a "noxious miasma," which is what they called the stench from the rotting coffee on Ball's Wharf.

A physician named William Currie didn't buy the stinky air theory.

He was convinced the fever had come on the ships carrying the Santo Domingo refugees. He believed the fever was contagious, that it spread from person to person.

Although the College of Physicians could not agree on the cause of the disease, doctors did agree to a set of guidelines for people to follow. These were published on August 27.

Some suggestions were common sense. Don't tire out the body or mind. Don't drink too much. Dress for the weather. Stop ringing the church bells every time someone died. The constant clang was terrifying people!

Other recommendations included, if you must leave the house, cover your mouth with a hanky dipped in camphor or vinegar. You were also encouraged to explode gunpowder in every room to clear your house of germs and inhale freshly ground pepper. People were told to cover the floors of their houses with 2 inches of fresh dirt and change it daily.

The number-one recommendation on the physicians' list sparked panic: stay away from infected people and places. People raced to escape the city, but as news of the fever spread, other communities slammed their doors. Nobody wanted the disease in their towns.

Winchester, Virginia, put a guard at every avenue into town and inspected people and packages for signs of infection. Lancaster, Pennsylvania, posted handbills that alerted people to the "Malignant Fever That Raged In Philadelphia."

A Delaware town attacked and sank a ship from Philadelphia. Manhattan sent $5,000 in aid, but refused to let anyone from Philadelphia inside New York City.

Despite this rude reception, 50 percent of Philadelphia's population abandoned the city, including its elected leaders.

———◆———

Politicians are human, too, and they were freaking out about yellow fever just like everybody else. When a new session of the Pennsylvania state legislature convened on August 27, only half the lawmakers showed up.

When the doorkeeper of the legislative chamber was found dead two days later, the politicians panicked. The legislature adjourned until December, and all state lawmakers, including Pennsylvania Governor Thomas Mifflin, left the city.

So much for the captain going down with the ship.

The federal government also fell apart. Alexander Hamilton, the head of the U.S. Treasury, got sick on September 5 and left town. Six out of seven Treasury Department clerks caught the fever, too. The nation's attorney general was out of town when the epidemic struck and his office quickly fell apart. When clerks for the U.S. Post Office got sick, the mail was not delivered.

Secretary of State Thomas Jefferson left for his Virginia estate as soon as the fever began to spread.

Epidemics and Pandemics

President George Washington claimed he wanted to remain in Philadelphia, but, "as Mrs. Washington was unwilling to leave me surrounded by the malignant fever . . . I could not think of hazarding her." On September 10, George and Martha Washington left for Virginia.

These exits put the country in a legal crisis.

In 1793, the federal government was barred from doing business anywhere except in the nation's capital. Now, that capital was contaminated. The federal government could not pass laws or pay its bills. The United States was in serious trouble.

The only elected leader who remained in Philadelphia throughout the crisis was Mayor Matthew Clarkson. Yellow fever had already killed his wife and youngest son, but Clark still stayed. Heroes sometimes appear where we least expect them.

———◆———

Yellow fever patient
painting by: Etienne Pariset and Andre Mazet

Yellow fever is brutal. The illness begins with fever, chills, severe headaches, muscle pain, nausea, and vomiting. Some people also have bloodshot eyes and a fuzzy tongue. Their pulse slows.

After three days, the fever breaks, and some patients recover. However, 15 to 20 percent of them get sick again within hours.

When this happens, the symptoms are much worse. The fever returns. The kidneys don't work properly, so the patient's skin turns yellow and they bleed from their mouth, nose, eyes, and stomach. The blood in the stomach is vomited up. People become delirious and hallucinate.

This is a sign that death is close.

With half of Philadelphia's population gone and the other half sick, dead, or barricaded inside their houses, the city shut down. Most of the newspapers stopped publishing, so citizens had few facts about what was happening. Farmers refused to deliver goods, so food became scarce and expensive.

Shops shuttered their windows and taverns locked their doors. The port closed down. All economic activity stopped, so people's income dried up, too.

Terror tore the community apart. People stayed home behind locked doors. If they had to go out, they wrapped their faces in vinegar-soaked scarves and walked down the middle of the street to avoid infected houses.

Some parents tossed their own children out on the street when the kids became sick. Children whose parents died roamed the city looking for food.

Those who could afford it, called the doctor. But sometimes, the cure was worse than the disease.

There were two treatment options for yellow fever—the traditional approach or the "heroic" method. Doctors disagreed strongly on which was more effective.

The traditional method for fever meant stimulating the body with sweet wine, quinine, and cold baths. But when Benjamin Rush used this approach and his patients kept dying, he researched his medical books. He discovered that in 1744, a doctor had called for a more radical approach.

This doctor said that since yellow fever patients had a large amount of blood in their bellies, this blood must be drained before it "putrefied."

Determined to force the disease out of his patients, Rush pioneered the heroic treatment. It involved a two-step process of "purging and bleeding." The name "heroic" fit because only a very tough person could endure such a cure.

A purge prescription might have read like this.

Take 10 grains of calomel (a white powder that contained the poison mercury) and 15 grains of jalap (a Mexican plant).

Stay close to the outhouse because you will vomit and expel waste frequently and violently.

Repeat three times daily.

Side effects: Bleeding colon, black teeth, excessive saliva

Caution: Avoid purging for too long because ingesting too much mercury can be fatal.

Step two of Rush's treatment was to bleed the patient. Bleeding was a common treatment for many ailments at this point in history. Doctors believed bleeding helped balance out body fluids. A doctor would cut open a patient's vein and drain a little blood into a bowl. Rush did not take a little blood— he took gallons.

Rush calculated the human body held 25 pounds of blood (the actual amount is half that). He recommended draining 60 to 80 ounces, almost half a person's blood supply.

Because of his reputation, people flocked to Rush's clinic to have their veins sliced. At the height of the epidemic, he and his five assistants treated more than 100 patients a day. They ran out of containers, so patients were treated in the street, their blood flowing down the cobblestones.

Some doctors ridiculed the heroic method, calling Rush the "Prince of Bleeders."

One physician called it a "prescription for a horse." Another said sarcastically that Rush had made "one of those great discoveries which have contributed to the depopulation of the earth."

But Rush stuck to his guns. He claimed his "cure" had worked 99 out of 100 times.

Now we know Rush was wrong. Historically, yellow fever kills about 20 percent of infected people. Of Rush's patients, 45 percent died. How many of those deaths were the result of his "heroic treatment" is not known, but extreme bleeding and purging couldn't have done them much good.

◆

Mayor Matthew Clarkson showed up at City Hall every day, but he was swamped. Sick beggars wandered the streets. When they dropped dead, their bodies lay on the street, sometimes for days. When someone could be found to haul the dead to a common grave, the poor were still denied a decent burial. There was a shortage of coffins and not enough grave diggers, so the corpses rotted in the sun.

The Overseers and Guardians of the Poor was a group responsible for caring for Philadelphia's poor people, but many of these guardians had fled the city. Mayor Clarkson told the remaining members to find someplace to house sick, poor people.

Bush Hill
painting by: James Peller Malcolm

Bush Hill was a vacant mansion two miles outside the city. Its owner was in England. Without any legal authority, the guardians seized the house and put yellow fever patients in every room, closet, and stairwell. Unfortunately, housing alone was not enough.

Bush Hill became a nightmare. Four doctors were assigned to tend the sick, but two of these physicians got sick themselves and the other two rarely showed up. Patients laid in their own excrement and vomit.

When the guardians put out a call for volunteers, only one medical student showed up. He described Bush Hill as "a great slaughter house" and stopped coming.

Mayor Clarkson decided extreme times call for extreme measures.

On September 10, the mayor published an appeal in the newspaper addressed to the "benevolent citizens." The city was desperate. Anyone healthy enough to lend a hand should come to City Hall to save Philadelphia. The mayor's call was answered by 26 men.

Ultimately, a committee of 12 volunteers took control of Philadelphia. They hired medical staff, purchased supplies, and organized the care of the sick and the burial of the dead. To pay for all this, the committee borrowed more than $37,000, a fortune in 1793.

The committee's actions were completely illegal. These people had not been elected and had no authority to borrow and spend money. No one knew what consequences they might face in the future. But the committee members did know that if they failed to act, Philadelphia would have no future.

Committee members combed the city. They hung red flags on houses with yellow fever, opened an orphanage for homeless children, and took over management of Bush Hill. Almost immediately, the committee realized they needed help.

But people were so afraid of yellow fever. Who would lend a hand? In early September, Dr. Benjamin Rush wrote to the Free African Society (FAS), a charity group formed by Absalom Jones and Richard Allen to help their fellow African Americans.

Rush told the group that God had granted black people immunity to yellow fever, so they should come to the aid of their white neighbors. Historians now believe that people who had grown up in an area with a lot of mosquitoes, such as West Africa, really did have higher levels of immunity, since they might have been exposed to the disease as children.

In 1793, about 3,000 free blacks and 200 slaves lived in Philadelphia. Their race meant they were often treated as second-class citizens. The FAS decided the epidemic was their chance to prove they were worthy of respect from whites.

Mayor Clarkson must have heaved a sigh of relief when Absalom Jones and Richard Allen told him to put FAS to work.

For the rest of the epidemic, Philadelphia's African-American population worked as nurses, cart drivers, street sweepers, grave diggers, and coffin makers. Dr. Rush even taught his bleeding technique to some members, who performed at least 800 bleedings.

While most white doctors refused to touch the nasty fluids coming out of yellow fever patients, black nurses washed bodies, bedding, and bathrooms. Twenty-one-year-old Isaac Heston said, "I don't know what the people would do if it was not for the Negroes."

On October 11, 119 deaths were reported to authorities. Two weeks later, the temperature fell below freezing. Mosquitoes went into hibernation. On October 31, a white banner was unfurled at Bush Hill that proclaimed, "No More Sick Persons Here." While people continued to die into December, the epidemic was over.

On November 10, without a word to his staff, President Washington rode alone into Philadelphia. Congress was due back in session in December, and the president wanted to know if the city was safe.

He was greeted by a very different city from the one he had fled two months before. The streets were clean and free of orphans and beggars, but the survivors of yellow fever looked like death's leftovers. They were thin, haggard, and reeked of vinegar. Peoples' skin was still slightly yellow and their teeth stained a dirty black.

During the crazy days of the epidemic, no one kept accurate records of how many people were dying, so an exact death toll is not known. Historians estimate yellow fever killed 5,000 people in 1793.

If yellow fever swept through Washington, DC, today with the same deadliness as it did in Philadelphia in 1793, 400,000 people would die in just three months.

◆

Even before the dying ended, the hateful accusations began.

Philadelphia publisher Mathew Carey attacked the African American community in a pamphlet published on November 14, 1793. He accused black nurses of plundering the houses of the sick and overcharging their white patients. The pamphlet quickly sold out and Carey printed three more editions.

Members of the FAS were furious. Absalom Jones and Richard Allen met Carey's charges head-on with a pamphlet of their own. The reason the rates of some black nurses skyrocketed was because white patients got into bidding wars for their services. Plenty of black nurses took care of sick whites for free.

Why didn't Carey mention the five white men who charged a family $43 to put a corpse into a coffin and haul it to a nearby wagon? Why didn't he talk about the white nurse found drunk and wearing her patient's jewelry? The real villains were Carey and other whites who had abandoned Philadelphia during the crisis.

Jones and Allen proved that African Americans suffered as much as whites during the epidemic. They published a "bill of mortality" showing that yellow fever killed as great a percentage of black people as it did whites.

It was the first document in United States history where members of a black community directly confronted white accusers.

When yellow fever finally left Philadelphia, fear stayed behind. Some people wondered if city life was just too dangerous. What would happen when the next epidemic struck? Would the government abandon its responsibilities again? Would neighbor turn on neighbor, parent on child?

Philadelphia answered these questions with bold, positive action. City leaders created a board of public health and transformed the dirty blocks along the waterfront into parks. Engineers built a new waterwork system that pumped water from the Schuylkill River into a wooden reservoir and gravity-fed it to houses and businesses.

Previously, wells were located close to outhouses, where human waste seeped into the drinking water. With the new system, the water tasted better and did not stink. Because water did not need to be pumped by hand, people bathed more often. That's progress.

While these improvements made life in Philadelphia better, they did not stop yellow fever. The disease returned repeatedly to cities across the United States.

Yellow Fever Threatens Independence

In 1900, a U.S. Army study led by Dr. Walter Reed finally proved that mosquitoes cause yellow fever. Reed conducted experiments where healthy volunteers were divided into two tents. One tent was filled with mosquitoes. The other tent was mosquito free, but volunteers slept in blankets soaked in the vomit of yellow fever patients. Neither group got much sleep, but only the people in the mosquito-filled tent became sick. Today, this study would be considered unethical.

Once people knew mosquitoes were the culprits, countries took steps to control them. Better sanitation systems, the elimination of standing water, and using pesticides cut down on the number of mosquitoes. In 1937, a vaccine for yellow fever was developed. Today, the World Health Organization promotes vaccination in Africa and South America, where the virus still sickens many.

The *Aedes aegypti* mosquito is a common pest in the southern part of the United States today. If a traveler from Brazil or Nigeria who was infected with yellow fever entered the United States and was bitten by one of these pests, history could repeat itself. No U.S. drug manufacturer has produced the yellow fever vaccine for years. If the disease invaded a large American city, it would take months to produce enough vaccine to supply the population. People would get sick. Some would die. Despite all the progress made since 1793, there is still no cure for yellow fever.

FORT DEVEN:

BOSTON, MA

PENNSYLVANIA

ILLINOIS

KANSAS ● CAMP FUNSTON

● HASKELL COUNTY

TEXAS

GEORGIA

1918
The Spanish influenza spreads across the globe at the end of World War I and causes the deadliest pandemic in history.

YOU
ARE
HERE

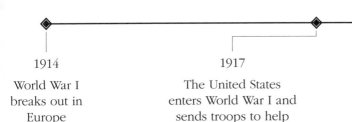

1914
World War I
breaks out in
Europe

1917
The United States
enters World War I and
sends troops to help
fight in the trenches

1918
The war ends and
the Spanish flu
spreads as people
move about the
globe

Chapter Four

Deadly Traveler: The Spanish Flu

In 1918, children chanted a rhyme
while they were skipping rope.

"I had a little bird.
It's name was Enza.
I opened up the window,
And In-flu-enza."

This kids' rhyme may sound sweet and innocent, but when you learn the history behind the little bird named Enza, you'll want to wring its neck.

All forms of influenza virus, or the flu, start in the digestive tract of birds. Usually, they stay there. Once in a while, however, a virus jumps species and infects a human. This is what happened in 1997, when humans became infected with the avian bird flu (H5N1 virus) in Hong Kong and the disease spread to other countries.

The good thing about avian flu is that it's passed from chicken to person, not person to person. So it's not likely to cause a global pandemic. Unless, of course, conditions are exactly right for the disease to develop and spread.

Which is exactly what happened in 1918.

Do you get flu shots every year? Many people get the flu in the fall or winter. When people become infected, they feel lousy for a week and then bounce back. The flu can kill, but it rarely does, and normally the only people at risk are the very young and the very old.

The year 1918 was anything but normal. That year, the clever little H1N1 virus not only figured out how to jump from bird to human, it also spread from person to person. A cough or sneeze was all it took. And back then, there was no flu immunization.

This 1918 flu was nasty. It attacked people deep in their delicate lung tissue, causing such severe inflammation that victims suffocated.

To make matters worse, this super-lethal, highly contagious virus appeared during World War I. Troops were on the move across the globe. Leaders were so concerned about waging war on each other that they downplayed the danger of the enemy in their midst. A global war, inadequate leadership, and a super virus conspired together.

The result? The deadliest pandemic in history.

In 1918, a man named Loring Miner doctored the hardworking, hearty people of Haskell County, Kansas. In this flat, treeless land, farmers cultivated wheat and tended livestock.

Miner rode hundreds of miles to make house calls. His patients trusted him, even though he drank too much. But alcohol wasn't muddling Miner's mind in the winter of 1918, when he saw a troubling pattern.

Patients were sick with violent headaches, body pains, high fevers, and dry coughing. Miner diagnosed influenza, but this flu was different from the typical strains. It moved from person to person with lightning speed and it killed. However, this flu didn't claim the usual victims—the very young and the very old.

The people dying were young adults in the prime of life.

In 1918, doctors were not required to report the flu to authorities. No state or public health agencies kept track of outbreaks. But Miner was so worried about this new flu that he contacted public health officials. His warning about "influenza of severe type" was published in March in a journal distributed by the U.S. Public Health Service. No one paid much attention.

Then, the illness abruptly disappeared. In a different time, the story might have ended right there. Not many people lived in Haskell County. H1N1 could have simply died out. But in 1918, American men from every state were enlisting in the army to join the fighting of World War I.

Camp Funston, Kansas, housed and trained 56,000 Army recruits. That winter, some soldiers from Funston received leave to visit their families in Haskell County. These men returned to camp the last week of February. On March 4, a soldier at Funston came down with the flu.

Within three weeks, 1,100 soldiers were in the fort hospital and thousands more lay sick in their cots. Thirty-eight men died. Still, authorities were not alarmed.

Every week, soldiers from Camp Funston were sent to other military bases and to the front lines of Europe. World War I was fought in mazes of trenches that zigzagged across Western Europe. Soldiers slept, ate, fought, and died in these ditches. The area called no-man's-land stretched between the enemy trenches and could be as wide as a football field or as narrow as 20 feet.

Deadly Traveler: The Spanish Flu

The soldiers from Camp Funston went to Europe armed with machine guns—and influenza—and began to kill.

◆

The United States had entered World War I reluctantly. President Woodrow Wilson was reelected to his second term in 1916 under the slogan, "He kept us out of the war." Five months later, Wilson changed his mind. Now, he wanted to go to war to "make the world safe for democracy."

photo credit: H.D. Girdwood

Not everyone agreed with Wilson, but the president was a man with razor focus and obsessive determination. Once he decided to wage war, nothing would get in his way.

The federal government cracked down on all opposition. The press was censored. The U.S. Post Office had the power to refuse mail delivery of any material it considered unpatriotic. It was illegal to say anything negative about the nation or its government.

To fire up patriotism, Wilson hired a man named George Creel to get people behind the war. Creel created an army of volunteers called Four Minute Men who gave short speeches before movies, meetings, plays, and concerts. They urged audiences to support the troops by buying government bonds, called Liberty Loans.

Creel also encouraged people to spy on each other. Anyone unwilling to buy bonds was harassed as a "slacker" or loser. Nothing would be permitted to interfere with the war effort or to hurt the morale of the troops or citizens.

Neither Wilson nor Creel counted on influenza.

———◆———

Deadly Traveler: The Spanish Flu

The town of San Sebastián, located on Spain's northern coast, was a popular tourist destination. It offered sun, surf, and, in 1918, peace. Spain was neutral during World War I, so tourists went there to escape the war. But in February 1818, influenza traveled to San Sebastián, too.

This version of H1N1 was not deadly, but it was fast-moving. A person was exposed one day, got sick two days later, and recovered three days after that. The illness infected 8 million Spaniards in two months, most of them young adults. The English-speaking media labeled the illness the Spanish flu.

That spring, the Spanish flu traveled to France and infected British, French, and American troops. Ignoring battle lines, the disease traveled to Germany and Austria-Hungary. So many soldiers on both sides were laid up that battle plans had to be changed.

During the war, ships moved men and material all around the world. Influenza traveled with them. Soon, the virus reached Asia.

Unlike the influenza that worried Dr. Miner in Haskell County, the Spanish flu was not deadly. Of the 613 American soldiers hospitalized in France that spring, only one died.

By early June, the flu was gone. Soldiers resumed shooting each other from the trenches.

———◆———

Influenza had not vanished, it had gone underground. It was mutating and swarming, preparing to explode on the world's stage.

There are three types of flu viruses—A, B, and C. Type A is the bad guy, the bug that can take down the world.

Influenza is endemic, epidemic, and pandemic. Endemic means the disease is always around. It visits almost every country every year. Influenza is often epidemic, too. This means the virus can cause widespread infection throughout an entire region. Sometimes, a city will close its schools for a day or two if too many students and teachers are sick. That's a city epidemic.

Pandemics are rare. These happen when influenza goes global. Pandemics are usually caused by new strains of flu. Because flu germs are airborne, they spread easily. If no one has immunities to a new virus strain, the illness travels like wildfire.

Viruses are strange creatures. They don't eat or burn oxygen or reproduce or make waste. They are more similar to a collection of inactive chemicals than a life form. A virus has one job—to make more of itself. But it can't do this alone, so it hijacks human cells.

A virus is a membrane, a kind of envelope with little spikes that jut out its sides. When the virus bumps up against a human cell, these spikes fit snugly against the molecules on the cell's surface. Like a hand slipping into a glove, the virus binds itself to the cell. Now, that cell is doomed.

The virus slips inside the cell, where it will be hidden. The body's defense system can't find the virus and kill it. The virus spills into the cell, replacing the cell's genes.

The virus barks orders: "Copy me! Copy me! Copy me!"

The human cell must obey. It replicates the influenza virus. Not just a few copies—hundreds of thousands of copies. These replicas explode out of the cell and invade the human's body. The whole process from cell attachment to cell explosion takes about 10 hours.

The process isn't perfect. A few virus copies aren't perfect duplications. Most of these mutations make it harder for the virus to infect its host. But now and then, a mutation will come along that gives the virus a superpower to adapt, infect, and spread.

Somewhere along the first wave of its journey in the spring of 1918, H1N1 mutated. When a second wave of virus struck, it was still very contagious, but now it was also lethal.

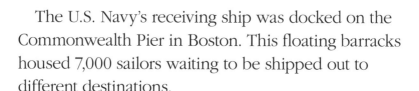

The U.S. Navy's receiving ship was docked on the Commonwealth Pier in Boston. This floating barracks housed 7,000 sailors waiting to be shipped out to different destinations.

The vessel was so overcrowded that sailors practically slept on top of each other and bumped elbows at the mess hall.

On August 27, 1918, two sailors reported to the sick bay with influenza. The next day, eight more showed up. On day three, 58 were sick and, by day four, the toll had risen to 81. On September 3, a civilian with the flu was admitted to Boston City Hospital.

About 35 miles away from Boston, on thousands of acres of rolling hills, stood Fort Devens. The military camp had been built to hold 36,000 men, but that September, more than 45,000 men were crammed inside. General John J. Pershing, the commander of U.S. troops in France, was desperate for men to put on the front lines of the war. Fort Devens was training these new recruits as quickly as possible in order to ship them to France.

The hospital at Fort Devens could house 1,200 people. There were 25 highly skilled doctors and a team of professional nurses to care for patients. The staff felt ready to handle any emergency.

They were wrong.

On September 1, four soldiers came down with what doctors diagnosed as pneumonia. During the next week, 22 more men sickened. One man was delirious and screamed when he was touched. Meningitis, the doctors concluded.

No one was quarantined.

Then, the situation exploded. In one day, 1,543 men reported sick with the flu. The camp's medical staff pleaded for help, and a small battalion of army and civilian doctors poured in to lend a hand. Soon, many of them were ill, too.

Symptoms varied. Patients described excruciating joint pain, sledgehammer headaches, high fever, vomiting, loss of smell, inflamed eyes, and a severe cough. Some patients had pockets of air under their skin, so when they rolled over, they crackled.

One nurse described the sound as similar to the snap-crackle-pop of Rice Krispies cereal.

Soldiers entered the hospital with brownish-blue spots on their cheekbones. Oxygen-rich blood is bright red, but unoxygenated blood is blue. These soldiers were suffering from cyanosis, a condition caused by a lack of oxygen in the blood. The cyanosis spread until the men looked "a dusky leaden blue" or an "indigo blue."

Patients bled from their ears, nose, mouth, and eyes. Some nosebleeds spurted several feet. Dr. Roy

Grist wrote a colleague on September 29 that, "One can stand to see one, two, or twenty men die, but to see these poor devils dropping like flies gets on your nerves."

Soon, Fort Devens was averaging 100 deaths a day.

The U.S. surgeon general ordered four of the nation's leading doctors to Fort Devens to diagnose this new disease. The men arrived on a cold and rainy September 23. Sick soldiers filed into the hospital, wrapped in blankets, their cheeks flushed with fever even as chills rattled their bones.

In the hospital, every room, hallway, and closet was crammed with beds. About 8,000 soldiers lay helpless, and many of their nurses were sick in cots beside them. The building reeked of sickness, urine, feces, and blood-stained sheets and clothing. Hacking and gagging echoed through the corridors.

Bodies were stacked "like cord wood."

The visiting doctors observed an autopsy of a young soldier. Every time his body was moved even slightly, liquid poured from the boy's nostrils. When his chest was cracked open, the doctors gasped. They were veterans who had treated infections of every kind, but this boy's blue and swollen lungs shot fear through their veins. Dr. William Henry Welch said, "This must be some new kind of infection . . . or the plague."

Soldiers from Boston and Fort Devens had already been transferred to naval yards in Philadelphia, Chicago, and New York. Others were headed to Europe and beyond. There was no way to rein in the unleashed virus.

———◆———

By the fall of 1918, 2 million American soldiers had arrived in France. Almost half of them disembarked at Brest, France. American soldiers mingled with troops from all around the world, and then they marched off across Europe.

They took influenza with them.

Freetown, Sierra Leone, is a port on the West African coast. It served as a coaling station for ships traveling from Europe to South Africa and Asia. On August 15, a ship with 200 sick sailors docked there. The infected men loaded coal and headed on their way. But before departing, they passed on influenza germs via every breath.

By the first week of October, influenza had spread worldwide. People in Ottawa, Canada, reported empty streetcars and deserted theaters. In Cape Town, South Africa, deaths came so fast the city ran out of coffins and people were buried in blankets.

In India, people could no longer cremate their dead because there was not enough wood to light millions of funeral fires.

The virus reached remote areas that rarely saw influenza. Inuit villages in Alaska almost became extinct.

When a team of doctors finally reached an isolated cluster of villages near Nome, Alaska, everyone had died in three of the villages and only 15 percent of the people survived in the others. Starving sled dogs had broken into igloos and fed on the corpses.

The remote Fiji Islands in the Pacific Ocean were also decimated. There, 14 percent of the population died in only 16 days.

Mexico, Brazil, China, Japan, Russia, Iran—influenza went almost everywhere. The virus skipped over the island of American Samoa, and Australia escaped with very few flu cases thanks to a strict quarantine around the continent. The rest of the world, however, suffered terribly.

In the early days of the outbreak, people thought the illness was just an army disease and life carried on. Women protested for the right to vote. Babe

Ruth helped the Red Sox win the World Series. In Philadelphia, thousands of people headed to Broad Street on September 28 for a Liberty Loan parade.

Few Philadelphians knew that the day before, 200 people had been admitted to the hospital for influenza, most of them civilians. Dr. Wilmer Krusen, the director of Philadelphia's Department of Public Health, was aware the flu had reached Philadelphia.

But he did not want anything to interfere with the war effort.

He told the board of health there was no epidemic among the civilian population, so the board simply issued some basic guidelines: no coughing, sneezing, or spitting in public, stay warm, keep feet dry and bowels open, and avoid large crowds.

Despite this last recommendation, Dr. Krusen refused to cancel the Liberty Loan parade. Dr. Howard Anders strongly objected, saying the parade was "a ready-made inflammable mass for a conflagration." He begged newspaper editors to caution people to stay home. But no paper wanted to be accused of not supporting the troops. The parade went on as planned.

Marching bands, Boy Scouts, military men, women's groups, and thousands of waving flags—the parade stretched for 2 miles. Two hundred thousand people lined the streets, pressing up against each other for a better view, cheering over each other's shoulders, shouting to friends nearby.

It was a picture of patriotism and disaster.

Two days after the parade, Dr. Krusen issued a statement: "The epidemic is now present in the civilian population." Indeed, it was. On October 1, 117 people died. The next day, every single bed in Philly's 31 hospitals was full.

On October 3, Krusen banned all public meetings, including Liberty Loan events. Schools, churches, theaters, and taverns were shut down.

Philadelphia's newspapers downplayed what was happening. After public meetings were banned, the *Philadelphia Inquirer* asked, "What are the authorities trying to do? Scare everyone to death?"

On October 5, when 254 people died, the papers reported that public health officials believed the epidemic had peaked. The next day, 289 people died.

On October 6, the *Public Ledger* insisted, "There is no cause for panic or alarm."

Cities and states got little guidance from the federal government. U.S. Surgeon General Rupert Blue made no effort to contain the illness even after he understood how fatal it was. Not until the end of September did the surgeon general finally issue a public warning.

He told people to avoid crowds, smother coughs and sneezes, breathe through the nose, and remember the three C's—clean mouth, clean skin, and clean clothes. He also recommended that people choose and chew their food well, wash hands before eating, avoid tight clothes, and, finally, "when air is pure, breathe all of it you can."

Later, Blue said he had not done more because he did not want to alarm citizens.

The crisis was also downplayed because no one wanted to be prosecuted for violating the law that barred people from interfering with the war effort. On September 26, the headlines in the *El Paso Herald* stated, "Vicious Rumors of Influenza Epidemic Will Be Combatted." In Chicago, the public health commissioner said he would "do nothing to interfere with the morale of the community" because "fear kills more than disease."

However, disease was killing plenty. The fatality rate in Chicago rose from 15 percent of flu victims at the start of October to 40 percent by month's end.

Newspapers that did print stories about the flu did not print helpful information. The *Albuquerque*

Morning Journal wrote a column titled "How to Dodge the Flu." Every day, it cautioned people not to let the flu frighten them.

The government and media might have thought they were keeping morale high and panic at bay, but the public wasn't stupid. Even as the newspapers urged calm, advertisements for the Red Cross stated: "The safety of this country demands that all patriotic available nurses, nurses' aides, or anyone with experience in nursing place themselves at once under the disposal of the gov."

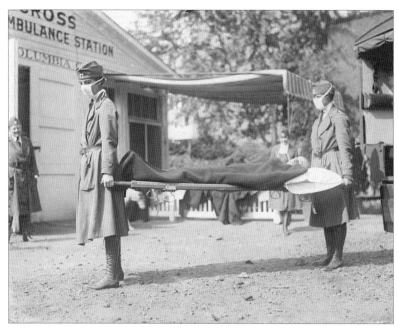

A demonstration by the Red Cross
during the Spanish flu epidemic
photo credit: National Photo Company

If everything was fine, why the urgent need for nurses? The public was afraid and it had reason to fear.

Concern about the war in Europe took a backseat to the flu. Americans went into isolation. People stopped talking to each other or even looking at each other. No more kissing and hugging or eating together.

In Prescott, Arizona, it was illegal to shake hands.

Many cities passed laws requiring people to wear face masks when they went out in public. These flimsy pieces of gauze could not fend off tiny viruses, and they created a creepy, faceless world.

Crepe paper was draped on houses where someone had died. Some people had to shield their eyes as they walked down the street because the sight of so much paper was too hard to bear.

Citizen committees that had been working to sell Liberty bonds a few months earlier now enforced anti-flu laws. In Phoenix, Arizona, if a person spit, coughed, or sneezed in public without covering their mouth, they could be arrested. Any business that remained open was required to provide 1,200 feet of cubic air space to each customer.

The rumor was spread that dogs caused the flu, so in Phoenix, police shot all dogs running loose in the city. Then, families began to kill their own beloved pets. There was no logic when it came to the flu.

◆

The army tried every weapon in its arsenal to halt influenza's spread. A soup of mucus and blood from flu patients was made into a vaccine, but all these shots accomplished were sore arms. Doctors made soldiers spray their throats with antiseptic. They hung sheets between patients' beds and strung them down the centers of tables in the mess hall.

The flu kept spreading.

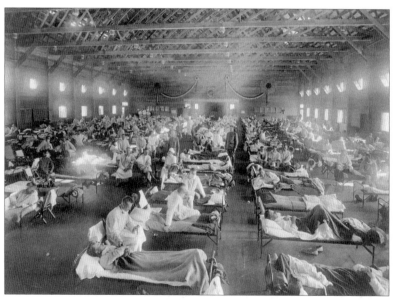

photo credit: Otis Historical Archives National Museum of Health & Medicine

Some doctors prescribed liquor. A half a bottle of wine, a shot of whiskey, a glass of port before bed—patients got drunk and still caught the flu. Newspapers advertised remedies such as Munyon's Paw Paw Pill and Oil of Hyomei for "bathing one's breathing organs."

All were a waste of money.

By October, undertakers could not keep up. Some hiked their prices by as much as 600 percent. In Philadelphia, there was a shortage of caskets. Many bodies had to wait days to be buried. People left their loved ones on front porches. People without porches kept the dead in a closed-off room. People with no extra room wrapped their family members in blankets and shoved them into corners.

In Philadelphia's morgue, the bodies were stacked four high in every room and along corridor walls. Covered only in blood-stained sheets with no refrigeration, the bodies created a stench that made people wretch.

Doors and windows were left open and children peeked in to see the gruesome sight. In the 31 days of October 1918, 195,000 Americans died, the deadliest month in the nation's history.

———————◆———————

Modern science didn't end the "Great Influenza Pandemic"—nature did. The virus simply ran out of victims. World War I ended on November 11, 1918, and by this time, infection rates had slowed dramatically.

However, influenza wasn't quite finished yet. In the winter of 1919, a third wave of illness struck. The virus had mutated yet again, so it was not as lethal, but people still died.

Finally, by spring 1919, the pandemic was over.

The Great Influenza killed between 8 and 10 percent of people aged 20 to 40. These were the college students, business owners, factory workers, mothers and fathers—people who should have survived. As kids, this age group had been exposed to a flu virus completely unrelated to H1N1. So when the Great Influenza struck, 20-to-40-year-old adults had no immunities, whereas younger kids and the elderly did.

Most flu viruses kill 0.8 percent of people they infect. In contrast, of the one-fifth of the global population that caught the Great Influenza, 2.5 percent of them died from it. That puts the death toll somewhere between 20 and 100 million people. Two-thirds of these deaths occurred in 24 weeks.

Deadly Traveler: The Spanish Flu

> Could such a deadly flu pandemic strike
> again? Scientists believe it will.

The best protection against a future flu pandemic
is vaccination. To make a vaccine, scientists
need some living virus, but the last victims
of the Great Influenza died in 1918, taking
the virus with them. However, in the 1990s,
researchers discovered preserved tissue of the
infected lungs of three influenza victims in a
small box stored in the Armed Forces Institute
of Pathology. Using these samples, scientists
recreated a monster—the 1918 influenza virus.

At the Centers for Disease Control in Atlanta,
Georgia, researchers are experimenting to
prepare for a possible pandemic. If the avian
flu virus mutated so people could spread it
to each other, the world would be in trouble.
Currently, scientists are combining the virus from
1918 with the avian flu virus to see if they can
engineer a disease spread by human contact.

These scientists aren't evil villains trying to
destroy the world. They must make the deadly
and contagious virus before they can develop
a vaccine to shield people from it. Maybe,
if the world is really lucky, in their work to
invent a vaccine, researchers will stumble
upon a cure so the flu can never kill again.

CANADA

UNITED STATES

SAN FRANCISCO

LOS ANGELES

ATLANTA

N
Y
C

MEXICO

HAI

1980s
A mysterious illness appears in the United States, but because it seems to target gay men, the government and the public don't respond with any urgency.

YOU ARE HERE

N
W E
S

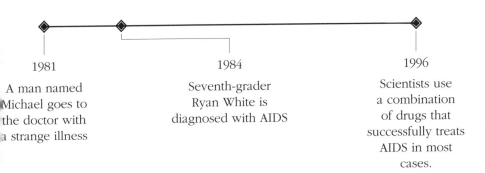

1981
A man named
Michael goes to
the doctor with
a strange illness

1984
Seventh-grader
Ryan White is
diagnosed with AIDS

1996
Scientists use
a combination
of drugs that
successfully treats
AIDS in most
cases.

Chapter Five

The Deadly Mystery: AIDS

The hunter crouched in the brush alongside the
Sangha River in southeast Cameroon. He was
hungry, always hungry. It was the late nineteenth
century. Every day, the white men made him
and the other African porters haul supplies
down miles of jungle trails to the trading post.

These white men, Germans, were greedy for ivory
from elephants and sap from rubber trees. From the
trading post, they moved the bounty down the great
Congo River to the Atlantic Ocean and on to Europe.

At last, a chimpanzee emerged from the jungle. It
waded into the river and then stopped, as if offering
itself to the hunter. He accepted the gift, slaying the
animal with one shot.

The hunter slung its carcass over his back. The chimp's dead weight rubbed against the sores on the man's shoulders, caused by the heavy pack he carried for the Germans. Blood from the wound on the chimpanzee's chest trickled down the hunter's back, seeping into his open sores.

The hunter ignored the blood. The only thing on his mind was silencing the rumble from his hungry stomach. The hunter carried his dinner back to camp, unaware of the destruction he was about to set loose on the world.

◆

A nameless virus had been killing chimpanzees in the Congo River Basin, but it did not affect people. However, when the blood of the chimp mingled with that of the hunter, the virus mutated. This mutation let the virus jump species. Now it could kill humans.

This was how human immunodeficiency virus (HIV) was born. HIV causes acquired immunodeficiency syndrome (AIDS), a disease with no cure.

If the hunter had been infected a few years earlier or a few years later, HIV might never have left the jungle. The part of Africa where the hunter lived was normally isolated, so the virus might well have died out before it jumped to other people.

However, timing is everything.

The hunter was infected with HIV during a brief window in history, between 1902 and 1921. During that time, Cameroon was a very busy place.

In the late 1800s, European nations used steamships, railroads, and guns to lay claim to most of Africa. It was a continent rumored to have vast treasures of gold and diamonds.

The city of Leopoldville, controlled by the king of Belgium, was located on the Congo River in a prime trading position. Europeans wanted the ivory in elephant tusks to make billiard balls, buttons, and bagpipes. They wanted the sap from the rubber trees for tires.

As the Germans shipped ivory and rubber from their trading post down to Leopoldville, HIV went along for the ride.

When Germany lost World War I in 1918, it also lost its African colonies. At the same time, the price of rubber collapsed. The window into the Congo River Basin that trade had opened was slammed shut.

But it was too late—HIV had already escaped the jungle. It lurked in Leopoldville, biding its time.

Leopoldville was the largest city in what was then called the Belgian Congo. Its population exploded from 49,000 people in 1940 to 400,000 by 1960.

Belgian officials helped HIV spread without even knowing it.

This happened as they gave shots to residents to protect them from tropical diseases. Sleeping sickness, caused by the bite of the tsetse fly, required a person to receive 36 injections during three years. Rather than buy tens of thousands of needles, health officials reused them. The few people carrying HIV passed it on to a few more through these needles.

Then, these individuals unwittingly handed HIV off to others. In addition to needles, the virus can jump from person to person through sex, from mother to baby during pregnancy and delivery and through breast milk. The virus works slowly, but eventually people developed AIDS.

Their symptoms of fever, diarrhea, and rapid weight loss were similar to so many other diseases in the region.

No one realized a new killer was on the scene.

Still, HIV might have stayed a local outbreak instead of becoming a global pandemic. However, when civil war broke out in the Congo in 1960, the United Nations sent 10,000 helpers to the Congo from Haiti, another French-speaking nation. One of these Haitians was infected with HIV while in the Congo. When he returned to Haiti, he brought it with him.

HIV had escaped Africa.

Haiti is fewer than 1,000 miles from Florida. HIV crossed this distance in someone's blood.

The virus might have been carried to the United States by an American tourist who visited Haiti. It might have arrived in a liter of blood donated from the Haitian center that supplied blood banks in Miami, Florida. Maybe it traveled in the body of a Haiti immigrant.

The exact scenario does not matter. What matters is that, by the 1970s, the AIDS virus had reached the United States.

Yet no one in the world even knew it existed.

In January 1981, Dr. Michael Gottlieb worked at the Medical Center in Los Angeles, California. He studied immunology, the branch of medicine that deals with how the body protects itself from infection.

A student brought Dr. Gottlieb the chart of a 31-year-old man named Michael who had an infection in his throat. This can be a sign of a sick immune system, but otherwise Michael appeared healthy. Dr. Gottlieb treated Michael's throat and sent him on his way.

Two days later, Michael was back. He was having trouble breathing.

Epidemics and Pandemics

Dr. Gottlieb took samples of Michael's lung tissue and discovered he had a very rare form of pneumonia. Dr. Gottlieb questioned Michael about his life, looking for clues about why such a strange infection would suddenly appear in a healthy man. Michael revealed that he was homosexual, but Dr. Gottlieb did not think that was important.

Determined to figure out the cause of Michael's illnesses, he sent a blood sample to the lab. The lab test discovered that Michael had no T-helper cells. These white blood cells are part of the body's immune system.

Dr. Gottlieb had never heard of a disease that specifically hunted down and destroyed white blood cells. After days of searching, Dr. Gottlieb remained stumped.

A few weeks later, another doctor sent a new patient to Dr. Gottlieb. This patient had a rash on his fingers, as well as other symptoms, such as diarrhea, high fever, and weight loss. Dr. Gottlieb felt a twinge of alarm and ran some tests. It was just as he feared. The man had the same rare pneumonia as Michael. He was also homosexual.

By the spring of 1981, Dr. Gottlieb had treated five patients with the same sickness, all gay men. Suddenly, this rare pneumonia was no longer rare.

It looked like the beginning of an epidemic.

Dr. Gottlieb's team reported the cases to the Centers for Disease Control (CDC) in Atlanta, Georgia. The CDC is the federal agency that tracks and works to stop the spread of disease across the United States.

The agency researched the pneumonia and discovered there had been only one case in the United States in the previous 15 years. Whatever was infecting Dr. Gottlieb's patients was something new.

That summer, 100 more unusual cases from Los Angeles, San Francisco, and New York were reported to the CDC. The patients were all gay men who also had a history of drug use. Some of these patients were covered in sores. They were walking skeletons. In really bad cases, the patients suffered terrible headaches and memory loss. They curled up in their hospital beds like frail old men and died.

Doctors could not figure out what had destroyed these men's immune systems. Doctors labeled the disease "gay-related immune deficiency," or GRID. Scientists were convinced that the cause of the disease was related to being gay.

Then, a new cluster of cases appeared and the mystery deepened.

———◆———

Dr. Margaret Fischl could not figure out what was making her patients sick. Every week, two to three Haitian immigrants came into her clinic in South Florida with skin and lung infections that did not make sense. Then, Dr. Fischl read about Dr. Gottlieb's cases and something clicked.

She called the CDC. "We think we're seeing the exact same thing in South Florida."

But when Dr. Fischl told officials that her Haitian patients weren't gay, they did not believe her. This illness affected only gay men, they told her. Agents from the CDC came down to interview Dr. Fischl's patients directly.

They asked the sick people offensive questions. What kind of strange rituals did they practice in Haiti? Are they sure they weren't gay?

One of Dr. Fischl's patients yelled, "I can't take this!"

Dr. Fischl ordered the agents to leave her clinic. The CDC wanted answers, but not the answers these patients were giving, because they did not fit the pattern the agents had already seen.

Soon, other evidence shed more doubt on the theory that the mystery disease affected only gay men. In New York, a doctor treated three men who were not gay, but who were drug users.

These addicts rented needles to inject heroin or cocaine into their bodies. Their needles were reused.

HIV infection rates exploded among New York drug addicts.

Then, Dr. Arthur Ammann diagnosed a toddler in San Francisco with the mystery illness. When the child was born, he had a sickness that was treated with blood transfusions. The baby got better and all was fine. But by the time the child was 17 months old, he kept getting infections. When Dr. Ammann examined the toddler, he recognized the symptoms of the new disease he had been reading about.

But this baby was not gay. He did not use drugs. He was not Haitian. What about the blood transfusions?

Dr. Ammann traced the list of people who had donated the blood the baby received. One was a 47-year-old businessman who had died in August. The newspaper said the man had died from "a long illness," and it listed his charity work and professional accomplishments.

The obituary didn't mention the man was gay. The "long illness" that killed him had been caused by an infection his body could not fight off because his immune system was helpless. He had the mysterious illness, and he had donated blood that had made the baby sick with the same illness.

Anyone in the country who needed a blood transfusion was at risk.

One group of Americans depended on blood transfusions for survival—hemophiliacs. Hemophilia is a rare disease in which a person's blood doesn't clot properly. Even small cuts can cause heavy bleeding that can be fatal. There is no cure for hemophilia, but people can live normal lives if they receive blood transfusions.

At this time in American history, blood bank centers across the nation paid people $10 for donating a pint of blood. Anyone could donate, including gay men and drug users. In 1982, the CDC began receiving reports of hemophiliac patients dying from this mysterious disease. Some of them were children. The need for action was urgent.

———◆———

This was one of the moments in the AIDS pandemic when the spread of the disease could have been slowed. But, for various reasons, it wasn't.

On July 27, 1982, the CDC held a meeting with people from the blood bank industry, gay rights organizations, and the hemophiliac community. The scientists laid out their evidence.

A new and deadly virus could be transmitted by blood. Certain groups of people—homosexuals, intravenous drug users, people of Haitian ancestry—must be prohibited from donating blood until more was known.

None of the groups believed the CDC's case *proved* anything. Homosexuals were major donors to the nation's blood supply. The gay community argued that singling them out was unfair. Hemophiliacs worried that fewer blood donations meant they wouldn't get the transfusions they needed to survive. The American Association for Blood Banks would lose millions of dollars if its blood supplies had to be dumped.

They said the CDC's "evidence was weak."

Dr. Don Francis from the CDC pounded the table. "How many more people do you want to kill! Do you want 10 dead? Do you want 20 dead? Do you want 100?"

The meeting was a failure. It would take two more years before safeguards to the nation's blood supply were implemented. During that time, 35,000 Americans were infected by contaminated blood.

The virus and the disease were renamed HIV and AIDS. Scientists had a name, but they needed to know much more about how this disease was transmitted and how to stop it.

In 1984, a medical team from the CDC went to the African nation of Zaire, the former Belgian Congo.

Many AIDS cases were being reported in the country, and scientists were stunned to find more than half of them were in women. It seemed that HIV could be transmitted through sex between men and women as well. If AIDS could be spread through heterosexual relations, it was a game changer. There were many more straight people on the planet than gay people.

As the pandemic grew, fear did too, usually fueled by ignorance and prejudice.

Barbara Fabian Baird was a nurse who cared for AIDS patients at the National Institutes of Health. She noticed that housekeeping staff and orderlies would only enter the room of an AIDS patient if they were gowned from head to toe. Food service workers set meal trays outside patient's doors instead of delivering them to the bedsides.

Baird was afraid, too. One day when treating a patient, she accidentally stuck herself with a needle. She went into the hallway and began to cry, afraid she had just signed her own death warrant.

The employee health services did not know how to help Baird. There was no treatment for AIDS in the early years of the epidemic.

The health service nurse told Baird, "I will . . . say some prayers for you." Luckily, Baird was never infected, but her fear was real.

There were few legal protections for AIDS victims in the 1980s. As news coverage of the epidemic spread, public hysteria did, too. AIDS patients were ordered to stay out of public restrooms. Cab drivers refused to give sick people rides. Hospitals put up signs warning people with AIDS not to enter.

People were fired from jobs, evicted from apartments, and kicked off medical insurance.

In 1986, Ricky, Robbie, and Randy Ray, three brothers with hemophilia, were barred from attending their elementary school in Arcadia, Florida. When a federal judge ruled the boys could return to school, an arsonist burned down the family's house.

Why was there so much aggression toward people with AIDS? The public might have responded with more compassion to the victims if their elected officials had led the way, but prejudice and ignorance guided their behavior, too.

In 1980, Ronald Reagan was elected president. This former Hollywood actor and governor of California pledged to cut the federal budget. He slashed the budget of the CDC by 25 percent. When the CDC assigned Dr. Don Francis to investigate the cause of HIV, he had no money to even set up a laboratory.

Dr. Francis said that for the first two years of the epidemic, "We . . . had nothing . . . we had to steal equipment from other laboratories. . . ."

The CDC pleaded for funds, but the government turned its back. In April 1983, Margaret Heckler, the head of the U.S. Department of Health and Human Services, told Congress that agencies researching AIDS had all the funding they needed. "I really don't think," Heckler said, "there is another dollar that could make a difference."

More money could have made a vast difference. But many people weren't willing to help homosexuals and drug addicts, AIDS's early victims Some people even believed AIDS was punishment for being gay. In 1986, Pat Buchanan, one of President Reagan's key advisers, said, "The poor homosexuals—they have declared war against nature, and now nature is exacting an awful retribution."

President Reagan did not speak publicly about AIDS until the epidemic had been raging for four years. Congressional Rep. Bill Dannemeyer called for a register of AIDS patients in case they needed to be quarantined or deported.

Other legislators scorned AIDS as "the gay disease."

———◆———

It took a movie star to soften some peoples' hearts to the terrible toll AIDS was taking on gay men. On July 15, 1985, Rock Hudson joined actress Doris Day at a press conference to promote Day's new television show. During the 1950s and 1960s, the handsome and funny Hudson had been a movie idol.

Viewers of the press conference saw a shadow of the former star. Rumors flew. What was killing Rock Hudson? Hudson gave his medical team permission to tell the truth. Doctors announced that not only was Hudson gay, he also had AIDS. Dr. Michael Gottlieb described the announcement as "a bombshell event."

The public began to realize just how widespread the epidemic had become.

President Reagan and his wife were both former actors who had been friends with Rock Hudson. In September 1985, the president finally spoke publicly about the epidemic. Health officials were hoping Reagan would assure people they could not get AIDS from casual contact. The president's words had the opposite effect.

Not once did Reagan use the word "AIDS." When asked if children with AIDS should be allowed to go to school, the president said that scientists had not yet proven "that it is safe. And until they do, I think we just have to do the best we can with this problem."

Public health officials came out immediately to reassure people that AIDS could not be spread through casual contact.

But the damage had been done. The parents in Russiaville, Indiana, heard the president's message that everyone was at risk and they were afraid.

That fear transformed into anger targeted against seventh-grader Ryan White.

Ryan was born with hemophilia and infected with HIV through blood transfusions. In 1984, he was diagnosed with AIDS and given six months to live.

Ryan told his mother, "They think I'm gonna die. You know what? They better not hold their breath." He lived more than five more years.

After his initial diagnosis, Ryan was out of school for more than a year. When his health stabilized in 1985, he tried to return to seventh grade. The school district superintendent refused, saying it put other people at risk. Ryan had to "attend" classes through the telephone.

Ryan sued the school, and, in 1986, the court ruled the district must admit him. However, the community was not welcoming. Some families withdrew their children and started an alternative school.

No one would hang out with Ryan. His home was vandalized. People on the street yelled at him when they saw him.

In 1987, the Whites moved to another town where the high school principal welcomed Ryan with a handshake. Life got better. Ryan worked a part-time job, went to the prom, and tried to live like an ordinary teenager.

But Ryan was not ordinary. His willingness to fight for his rights drew national attention, and Ryan became a spokesman for people living with AIDS. He gave television interviews and led fundraisers and testified before a presidential commission.

On April 8, 1990, Ryan White died at age 18. A few months later, President George H.W. Bush signed the Ryan White Care Act. This law provides funding to organizations that care for poor people suffering from AIDS and their families.

Attitudes about AIDS were slow to change, and science was, too. By 1990, more than 50,000 Americans had contracted AIDS and more than 40,000 had died.

Meanwhile, the pandemic had spread to every continent except Antarctica.

◆

One day in 1987, a man named Larry Kramer wrote down the names of people he knew who had died of AIDS. The list ran in the hundreds. "People really were dying like flies," Kramer recalled.

Kramer was sick of how things stood. The medical establishment had few answers. In 1985, a test was developed to detect HIV in blood and the nation's blood supply finally began screening donors.

However, there was still no good treatment for AIDS and no cure in sight.

The public treated AIDS patients as if they had the plague. A *Los Angeles Times* survey in 1987 showed that 50 percent of American people thought AIDS patients should be quarantined and 29 percent thought they should be tattooed so they were easily identified. The federal government refused to fund AIDS research enough to meet the growing crisis.

In early 1987, Kramer founded the AIDS Coalition to Unleash Power (ACT UP). The group, whose members were mostly gay men, engaged in large-scale protests. These acts of civil disobedience aimed to get the country's attention. ACT UP was nonviolent, but it was loud and angry.

ACT UP's first target was the U.S. Food and Drug Administration (FDA). The FDA took years to approve new AIDS drugs, even as people kept dying.

On March 24, ACT UP hung an effigy of the chairman of the FDA while chanting, "Ronald Reagan, your son is gay. Put him in charge of the FDA!"

Shortly after this, the FDA announced it would shorten its drug approval process by two years.

That same year, the first anti-HIV drug was approved by the FDA. This drug, called AZT, cost $10,000 per year, far too expensive for AIDS victims who didn't have health insurance.

To protest the high cost of the drug, some ACT UP members put on suits and wore fake IDs and snuck into the New York Stock Exchange. These men chained themselves to the balcony.

AIDS quilt
photo credit: National Institutes of Health

At 9 a.m., when the opening bell rang to start financial trading for the day, the activists set off fog horns. Within a few weeks, the company that made AZT lowered its price to $6,500 a year.

Peter Staley, a leader of ACT UP, said, "You have to have a war mentality. . . . If you stop to spend a lot of time on mourning, you'll lose the war. We prefer to skip the mourning stage and go straight to anger." The group's slogan was "Silence = Death."

The AIDS quilt was a quieter protest, but no less powerful. Gay rights activist Cleve Jones thought of the idea of a memorial quilt. He founded the NAMES Project Foundation with other activists.

In October 1987, the AIDS quilt was displayed for the first time on the National Mall in Washington, D.C. The quilt had 1,920 panels, each bearing the name of someone who had died of AIDS. Today, the quilt weighs 54 tons and has 44,000 3-by-6-foot memorial panels. The AIDS quilt is the largest community art project in the world.

In 1996, scientists finally developed a series of drugs that transformed AIDS from a death sentence into a lifelong disease. HIV never leaves the body, but with the right mix of medicines, the virus can be held in check so AIDS does not develop. This drug treatment slowed the epidemic in the United States, and deaths from AIDS began to decline during the late 1990s.

When the twenty-first century dawned, 95 percent of new AIDS cases were in countries too poor to afford the expensive new drugs that were saving the lives of Americans.

Today, the international community is trying to slow the spread of AIDS, but results are mixed. In 2015, 17 million patients were receiving life-saving drug treatments, but these drugs cover only 46 percent of the world's infected people. AIDS-related deaths have declined from 1.5 million people in 2010 to 1.1 million in 2015. That is a major improvement, but still too high a death toll. The United Nations has set the target of having 90 percent of HIV-infected people receiving treatment by 2020. However, the rates of infection remain high in Eastern Europe and Asia, especially among females ages 15-24.

The hope for the future lies with a cure or a vaccine. No one knows when, or if, that day will arrive. Seventy-five million people have been infected with HIV since the pandemic began and 35 million have died from AIDS. Fear and prejudice made the history of this pandemic one of missed opportunities. The terrible legacy of the hunter and the chimpanzee continues to impact millions of people, with no clear end in sight.

Glossary

acquired immunodeficiency syndrome (AIDS): a disease that attacks the body's immune system.

ally: united for a common goal.

ambush: a surprise attack.

anti-Semitism: prejudice or hostility toward Jewish people.

antibiotics: a substance that destroys bacteria or stops it from growing.

apocalypse: an event involving destruction or damage on a catastrophic scale.

apprentice: someone who learns to do a job by working for someone who already does the job.

aqueduct: a channel for moving water, usually in the form of a bridge over a valley.

arboviral: a group of viruses transmitted by mosquitoes and ticks.

architecture: the style or look of a building.

arsenal: a collection of weapons.

astrology: the study of how movements of the sun, moon, and planets affects humans.

bacteria: tiny microbes that live in animals, plants, soil, and water. Bacteria are decomposers that help decay food. Some bacteria are harmful to humans and others are helpful. Singular is bacterium.

bile: digestive fluid produced by the body.

blood bank: a place where blood is collected from donors to be used for people who need blood.

bloodletting: removing a person's blood as a medical treatment.

breed: to produce babies.

brigantine: a two-mast sailing ship.

bubo: a swollen, inflamed lymph node in the armpit or groin.

bubonic plague: a deadly infectious disease carried by rats and mice that can spread to humans. Also called black death.

cargo: goods or materials that are carried or transported by a vehicle.

catapult: a large war machine used to hurl objects at an enemy.

causeway: a raised road across wet ground or water.

censor: when the government examines material for the public, such as books, newspapers, or the news, and removes information it does not approve of.

cesspool: a place full of human waste.

chamber pot: a large, bowl-shaped pot used as an indoor toilet.

Christian: a follower of Christianity, one of the world's largest religions, who believes that Jesus Christ is the son of God.

Christianity: a religion based on the teachings of Jesus Christ. Followers are Christians.

civil disobedience: the refusal to obey laws as a form of peaceful protest.

civilian: a person not in the armed services.

colony: an area that is controlled by or belongs to another country. Also a group of something.

conquer: to defeat someone or something.

conquistador: Spanish conquerors of the Americas in the 1500s.

conspiracy: a secret plan among two or more people to do something wrong or harmful.

constellation: a group of stars that form a recognizable pattern or design.

contagion: an unseen particle that is infectious.

contagious: an easily transmittable disease.

contaminate: to pollute something.

Continental Army: the army of America during the Revolutionary War.

convert: to persuade someone to change their views.

convoy: a group of vehicles traveling together.

corpse: a dead body.

cultural: relating to the behaviors, beliefs, and way of life of a group of people.

decay: to break down and rot.

decomposer: an organism, such as a worm or ant, that breaks down dead and rotting organisms.

deport: to expel a person from a country.

diagnose: to determine the identity and cause of a disease.

diplomacy: talks between countries to solve differences.

discriminate: to unfairly treat a person or group differently from others, usually because of their race, gender, or age.

Glossary

disease: a sickness that produces specific signs or symptoms.

disembark: to get off a ship or plane.

distinctive: an aspect of something that makes it stand out as special or unique.

dormant: in a state of rest or inactivity.

economy: the way goods and services are bought and sold in a society.

effigy: a model of a person made to be destroyed as a form of political protest.

empire: a group of countries, states, or lands that are ruled by one ruler.

endemic: always around.

epidemic: a disease that spreads widely across a specific region during a certain time.

evolve: to change or develop gradually.

excrement: human or animal waste.

expel: to drive or push out.

exposure: being unprotected from the extremes of the outdoors, such as the cold and snow or the heat and sun.

feces: poop.

First Continental Congress: a meeting of delegates from the original 13 American colonies in 1774.

Florentine: a native or resident of Florence, Italy.

forearm: to prepare.

forewarn: to be warned of danger.

galley: a low, flat ship with sails and oars.

gender: male or female, and their roles or behavior defined by society.

gene: part of what controls a cell's characteristics.

ghetto: a section of a city inhabited by one minority group.

global: relating to the entire world.

gondola: a flat-bottomed boat used on canals in Venice, Italy.

groin: the area of the body above the thighs.

hemophilia: a medical condition in which a person's blood does not clot properly.

heterosexual: a person who is sexually attracted to others of the opposite gender.

hold: the part of a boat below the deck.

homosexual: a person who is sexually attracted to others of the same gender.

hygiene: the things people do to keep their bodies and surroundings clean and in good health.

ice age: a time in history when much of Earth was covered in ice.

ignorance: a lack of knowledge or information.

immune: resistant to certain infections.

infect: to contaminate.

infection: the invasion and multiplication of microorganisms such as bacteria and viruses that are not normally present within the body.

infectious: illness that is caused by bacteria or viruses that is able to spread quickly from one person to others.

infest: to live in or on in great numbers.

inflammation: when part of the body becomes reddened, swollen, hot, and often painful, especially as a reaction to injury or infection.

influenza: a contagious infection caused by a virus. Also called the flu.

intravenous: in the veins.

Jew: a follower of Judaism, one of the world's oldest religions.

Judaism: the religion developed by ancient Hebrews who believed in one god and that uses the Torah as its sacred text. Followers are Jews.

larvae: the worm-shaped form of a young insect (such as a caterpillar) before it becomes an adult.

latrine: a bathroom that can be used by several people at once, often as simple as a long trench dug in the earth.

lethal: deadly.

livestock: animals raised for food and other products.

lymph node: a small swelling in the lymphatic system of the body.

malevolent: having or showing a wish to do evil to others.

malignant: very infectious.

massacre: the brutal killing of a large number of people.

medieval: describes the Middle Ages, the period of European history after the fall of the Roman Empire, from about 350 to 1450 CE.

merchant: someone who buys and sells goods.

messiah: a promised savior and deliverer.

metropolis: a large city.

microbe: another word for microorganism. Viruses and bacteria are microbes.

microorganism: a living thing, such as a bacterium, that is so small it can be seen only with a microscope. Also called a microbe.

Glossary

Middle Ages: the period of time between the end of the Roman Empire and the Renaissance, about 350 to 1450 CE.

monarch: a ruler such as a king or queen.

monk: a member of a religious community.

morale: the confidence of people.

morgue: a place where bodies are kept.

mortality: death on a large scale.

mutate: to change.

nervous system: a body system that includes the brain, spinal cord, and nerves.

New York Stock Exchange: the building in New York City where stocks and bonds are traded.

nomad: a person with no permanent home who travels from place to place in search of food.

obsidian: volcanic rock.

optimism: hopefulness and confidence about the future.

organism: a living thing.

outbreak: a sudden, violent start of something.

pallet: a cushioned sleeping surface.

pandemic: when a disease infects many people in many countries at the same time.

patriotism: strong support for one's country.

peasant: a farmer in feudal society who lived on and farmed land owned by his lord.

peninsula: a piece of land that juts out into water.

pestilence: a fatal epidemic disease, especially bubonic plague.

plummet: to fall quickly.

pneumonia: a lung infection found in people with a weak immune system.

pneumonic: describes pneumonia, a lung inflammation.

population: all of the people (or plants or animals) in an area or in a group.

porter: a person who carries luggage or supplies.

poultice: a soft, usually heated substance that is spread on cloth and then placed on the skin to heal a sore or reduce pain.

prejudice: an unfair feeling of dislike for a person or group, usually based on gender, race, or religion.

prey: to hunt. Also animals hunted by other animals.

Glossary

prophecy: a prediction of the future.

purge: to get rid of something.

pustule: an inflamed blister full of pus.

quarantine: to isolate someone for a period of time after he has been exposed to an infectious disease.

queasy: to feel sick to the stomach.

quinine: medicine made from a certain kind of tree bark, which is used to treat malaria.

refuge: a place that gives protection.

refugee: someone who flees to escape war, persecution, or disaster.

remedy: a cure.

renaissance: a cultural rebirth. The Renaissance was a period of time in Europe after the Middle Ages, from the 1300s to the 1600s.

reservoir: a supply of something. Also a host, such as an animal, plant, insect, or person, that maintains, but does not get sick from, a bacteria or virus.

ricochet: to rebound one or more times off a surface.

ritual: a religious ceremony.

sacrifice: the killing of a person or animal as an offering to a god.

sanitation: conditions relating to public health and cleanliness.

scapegoat: a person or group who bears the blame for others.

scientific method: a method to test a theory that involves observing, measuring, and testing data.

sewage: waste from buildings, carried away through sewers. A sewer is a drain for waste.

shun: to avoid or reject.

siege: a military operation where the army surrounds a city, cutting off supplies to force the trapped people to surrender.

skeptical: questioning and not easily convinced.

slaughter: to kill.

smallpox: a deadly disease that leaves the skin scarred.

social: living in groups.

society: an organized community of people.

Spanish flu: the name of the influenza that caused the flu pandemic of 1918–1919.

species: a group of living things that are closely related and produce young.

stalk: to quietly follow prey.

steppe: a large area of flat, unforested grassland.

stowaway: something that hides aboard a vehicle to get a free ride.

suffocate: to kill or destroy by cutting off access to air or oxygen.

superstition: beliefs that deal with non-scientific things, such as good and bad luck.

T-cells: white blood cells that are part of the body's immune response.

technology: the tools, methods, and systems used to solve a problem or do work.

territory: an area of land.

thatch: straw, leaves, or any similar material used for making a roof.

theory: an unproven idea used to explain something.

trade: the exchange of goods for other goods or money.

transfusion: transferring donated blood into a person.

tribute: payment made by one government to another as a price for peace or security.

tumor: a growth or group of cancer cells.

vapor: smoke or steam.

vector: an organism that transmits a disease from one person to another.

villain: a character who does bad things.

virus: a microorganism that cannot grow or reproduce outside of another organism's cell.

wattle: sticks and straw filling the spaces between logs.

woo: to seek the favor of someone.

yellow fever: a tropical disease that causes fever and is often fatal. The virus is transmitted by mosquitoes.

Yersinia pestis: the bacteria that causes the bubonic plague.

Resources

Books

Anderson, Laurie Halse. *Fever 1793.* New York: Simon & Schuster, 2002.

Giblin, James Cross. *When Plague Strikes: The Black Death, Smallpox, AIDS.* New York: HarperCollins, 1995.

Murphy, Jim. *An American Plague: The True and Terrifying Story of the Yellow Fever Epidemic of 1793.* New York: Clarion Books, 2003.

Peters, Marilee. *Patient Zero: Solving the Mysteries of Deadly Epidemics.* New York: Annick Press, 2014.

Peters, Stephanie True. *Smallpox in the New World.* New York: Benchmark Books, 2005.

Articles

Read an article from CNN on different "patients zero" through history.
cnn.com/2016/11/08/health/patient-zero-history-super-spreaders/index.html

What do diseases have to do with fashion? Find out in this article from *Smithsonian Magazine.*
smithsonianmag.com/science-nature/how-tuberculosis-shaped-victorian-fashion-180959029

Videos

Watch a "Crash Course" video about deadly diseases in history.
youtube.com/watch?v=1PLBmUVYYeg

Learn more about the Spanish flu pandemic with this video.
youtube.com/watch?v=B6iuF6oOejI